CONTENTS

Out of England

TIMOTHY BULL

Rob

Best wishes!

Lin

ISBN: 978-1-0903-2433-7

INTRODUCTION

This is a story about my father. My story, just one of many that could be told about him.

His name was John, ordinary enough but that was the name he wanted people to use. He was christened Daniel John and his own family called him Jack. I call him, called him, Dad. There was something told about his being named after Daniel in the lion's den. At least I think so, I can't be sure, it's just one of those things which are half-seen through the mud of memory, like a lost gold ring. Along with his name he is numbered, he has dates: 1922 to 1992. Dad was born in the same year as the founding of the BBC and he died during the Royal Family's *annus horribilis*. Not that anyone knew it at the time, 1922 is now thought to be the year when the British Empire was at its peak of power and influence. For me, born almost forty years later, 1922 is the deep past, but 1992, the year of his passing, is more accessible. It marks the birth of my own second child who might have arrived in time to be loved by her grandfather if it were not for the indifference of three short months.

Her generation's world is routinely described as unrecognisable to its ancestors. So much has passed, so

1

much has changed. This sense of impenetrability troubled me when I set about telling Dad's story. I wanted it to be faithful, honouring, and truthful, but would I be able to find the man who is now eternally out of reach by following shadows and breadcrumbs? He was an ordinary man who left no diaries, no letters. The world of his generation, it is said, is gone. The map is no longer pink, the imperial chapter has closed and Britain is Something Else. The telegram boy's whistled tune has given way to Spotify. The tenant's doffed cap is redundant and his cottage is the National Trust gift shop. Leave and Remain have elbowed aside our certainties and left them stumbling. Even the year of Dad's passing, 1992, already looks like another country, doesn't it?

Yes and no. The islands and territories we call the United Kingdom are still here, surrounded by the same waters that bore our ships and our people to every continent, where they explored and built, killed and were killed, negotiated and deceived, and worked, worked, worked. What came out of it all, and eventually crystallised into something with the deceptive appearance of permanence, was the thing we called the Empire. With hindsight we know it was far from permanent, never could have been, yet its imprint endures in countless ways across those lands 'we' ruled. In legal and political systems, in language and customs which the British left behind when they retreated from their colonies, dominions, protectorates and dependencies, there is an imprinted legacy. I say this only to make the point that the world of the twenty-first century stays connected to those earlier times. This is reassuring; it meant I had a breath of a chance to navigate my way back through the past and find Dad's story.

***

It's mid-afternoon on a weekday in December, just a few days before Christmas, and outside there is a sky like a damp blanket. Inside I already have the lights on. On the wall above my desk is a framed map: The World, Political, Van Der Grinten Projection. The scale of the map means that Great Britain is about the size of a thumb-print while New Zealand, down there in the bottom right-hand corner, is as long and thin as my little finger.

Africa is bang in the middle of the map and if you look part-way down the bottom half of the continent – in the middle and far from the pale blue of the ocean – there is a country shaped like a deformed embryo. It is the place where I was born, sixty years ago. On my map it is marked out in pink; neighbouring countries have their own colours, orange and blue, yellow and green. To the left is Angola stretching west to the coastline where the Portuguese first planted their feet eight years before Columbus arrived in the New World. To the right Tanzania and Mozambique reach eastward, with little Malawi and its skinny lake tucked in behind. Massive and dominating, the Democratic Republic of the Congo pokes a penetrating finger from the north-west into the belly of my pink birthplace. Zimbabwe holds up the southern border, keeping at bay Botswana and Namibia in the south west.

Zambia. Dad had already been in Africa on and off for over seven years when he first went to the country and in those days it was called Northern Rhodesia. At that time I was yet to be born and as far as I know there were no plans to produce me. Dad already had a wife and two other sons, my older brothers. I have a black-and-white picture of them all from around that time. It is a photocopy of a snap that I found in an old family album and it is now stuck to my map, blu-tacked over a bit of Antarctica. Mum, who was called Doreen but insisted that she be called Dawn, is in matching skirt and jacket and a white blouse, with a black belt clipped around her narrow waist. She is holding a dachshund who stares obediently towards the camera. Dad is in dark trousers - slacks - and a light-coloured jacket with a shirt and tie under a V-neck jumper. My grinning brothers, Tony and Stewart, look like they were around the ages of seven and five when the picture was taken. Even they are wearing shirts and ties. This was, after all, the 1950's.

The background is unmistakably Africa. Despite the poor quality of the copy there is something about the bare dirt road and the shape of the trees and the intensity of the light. Another figure completes the group, standing next to Dad. I recognise her as Nan Stewart, Mum's mother. I only met her a few times, many years later in England, and I find it hard to imagine that she ever spent time in Africa. Dad hardly ever mentioned it, but over the years I picked up enough to know that Nan's presence there might explain why the camera captured a certain stiffness in the three adults, a contrast to the innocent faces of the boys.

I have some other pictures stuck to the map and obscuring more of Antarctica and part of Australia: Dad, grinning and painfully young in the uniform of the Royal Marines with his beret cocked to the very back of his head. In this one he looks a lot like my son and even more like my nephew and he can't have been much more than twenty-two. It was taken just before or after the allied invasion of Sicily. Another photo from wartime has Dad looking a bit less casual, standing in front of a hedge in his battledress with one arm around Mum and the other behind his back, Prince Philip style. Mum looks about sixteen but she must have been older, yet still not in her twenties. And there is one more of Dad which was taken much later, around 1968, and this one brings him into my own conscious life, the basket of my memories. He is sitting at a wooden government-issue desk with his name-plate prominent in front of a big blotter. He is writing, or pretending to write for the pose. You can see all the paraphernalia of an office from those times: the bulky black telephone, a pot of ink, wire IN and OUT trays and a shelf loaded with box-files. Behind Dad's right shoulder the sunlight reflects on the metal bars of the window and outside there is the dark silhouette of a tree.

You can't see it in the picture, but I know that two red fire-buckets hung from that tree, one filled with sand and one with water, and I once found an enormous caterpillar drowned in the water bucket. It was so big and fleshy and bloated that it frightened me. Memories like that, sometimes connected and sometimes not, are the threads of Dad's story. I have tried to draw them together and here and there I think I have succeeded. I have stared at dozens of photographs and I have dug up what I can from the meagre scraps of family record. Nobody kept any diaries. I have read books of history and politics and memoir – most of them out of print these days - and sometimes I have literally squeezed my eyes shut to force more fragments of memory to the surface.

One day I tried to find something erudite that a clever or famous person might have said about the subject of memory. Pretentiously I thought it would add a bit of gravitas to the story. One of the quotations Google popped up was spoken by a character called Bao Bomu, from Amy Tan's novel The Bonesetter's Daughter. She asks: 'what is the past but what we choose to remember?' It's a neat quote but it doesn't help. Unlike Bao Bomu I believe my own memories arrive unbidden, unchosen. They simply come, like gate-crashers. Some of them are just plain trivial, like the never-forgotten licence plate number – BH 8795 – on the white Volkswagen which Dad drove in Zambia in the late sixties. Or the picture of a deep, narrow hole in our lawn in Salisbury, now Harare, into which my brothers would squirt water from a hosepipe, waiting for a horde of frogs to emerge so they could carry them indoors and race them against each other in the bath.

Perhaps that is what a life is made of, a string of trivialities joined here and there by the occasional big event, all carried on against a backdrop of national and global goings-on. That backdrop constitutes the daily context for our lives which solidifies, like cooling wax, into the thing we call History. Some of the public events that marked out Dad's life were readily retrieved from my store of memory, decades later. I am old enough to remember the day, 24th of October 1964, when the Crown Colony of Northern Rhodesia became the Republic of Zambia and the Union Jack was lowered for the last time. I was six years old. More than fifty years later, that event appears pre-ordained, one more step in the march of change that was sweeping the old European possessions, but in the day-to-day of Dad's life in the nineteen-forties and fifties it would have seemed far from inevitable. It takes a conscious act of imagination to put ourselves into the heads of our forebears half a century ago and try to see the world the way they saw it. And it takes homework. To do it I needed more than a handful of childhood memories.

Thankfully there was a lot more information 'out there' than I imagined. Books, archives and social media have allowed me to connect with people and events from distant times and places. I have met with Dad's surviving siblings and with some of his friends and associates I had not seen or heard of for years. They have helped me to fill in a few of the blanks and put colour and texture into Dad's life, not only by closing gaps in my knowledge about people and places but also by offering explanations, connections, motives. I have read or listened to a string of family narratives about other men and women, strangers unknown by my family but who, like Mum and Dad, travelled to southern and central Africa in the middle of the last century and found their lives permanently marked by the experience. Most of them came from Britain. Many eventually returned to their home country while others sought to recreate their lives elsewhere, chasing the sun. Wherever they finally landed they carry a longing, almost without exception, for the red African soil.

I return to my map again and again and try to imagine

them all, those people. Wandering here, settling there. It has changed, their world – the names on the map show it - but the oddity of the imperial borders remains. For good or ill a mark has been left on the continent of Africa. It has been stamped with a visible reminder of the great imperial project.

My Dad was a tiny part of all that, but his life didn't start there.

ONE

Harold, Jesse, Edward, Kath, Jack, Violet, Daisy, Titch, Jean and Ron. Dad's name sits near the middle of a string of ten sisters and brothers. Harold, the eldest and named after his father, was born in 1915 in the midst of a war and baby Ron arrived in 1935 when they were still hoping to avoid another. Little Edward was struck down by diphtheria and didn't survive long enough to go to school. Some of the names they used for one another are not the ones recorded on their birth certificates; only Dad's family ever called him Jack while Titch was really called Dorothy and Jean was actually Edith.

Their parents had married on a warm and sunny day in August 1913, after a five-year courtship. Esther Hodges was only fifteen when she first met Harold Augustus Gillingship Bull in Orpington, Kent, the town of her birth. That was in 1908 – Edward VII was on the throne – and it was the first day off allowed to her from her new job as a housemaid. She was one of around 1.3 million domestic servants employed in Britain at that time. Nineteen year-old Harold, her future husband, was delivering groceries that day. He had been taken on at the age of thirteen by the food wholesalers C.C. Ryan Limited and he worked for them, uninterrupted, for fifty-eight years.

The young couple set up home in nearby Bexleyheath, close to Harold's workplace and where, as an outsider from Hackney, he had been lodging before he married. Within a year of their wedding the country was at war with Germany. Yet, as the conflict dragged out and millions of Harold's contemporaries were being shipped across the channel to mud and slaughter in France, he was told that his occupation in the food industry was considered to be of such national importance that he would be exempted from conscription. Had it been otherwise, I might not be here. Instead of fighting the Hun, Harold took advantage of his good fortune and his wife's natural fertility and started to sire that long list of babies – a twenty-year project and a monument to Esther's stamina and devotion.

Measured against the relative affluence of subsequent generations of Bulls I suppose we would have called them 'poor' but in those days, within the established layers of class and income, they probably saw themselves as quite comfortably off. They had a rented roof over their heads and a benevolent landlord. There was hot food on the table and coal in the grate. The semi-detached houses they occupied – three homes in their entire married life – seem ridiculously small for such a large family but somehow they all squeezed in. Esther's skill and economy as a home-maker and Harold's austerity combined to keep the wolf from the door; Dad remembered few extravagances. And rarely was there alcohol in the house or ever, probably, nights out at the pub. They avoided the expense and misery which that particular vice could bring to a family.

Not that keeping afloat was achieved without constant effort. For a while my grandmother had a small-scale enterprise selling fruit and vegetables from the side of the house. There must have been a connection to her husband working in the grocery trade, but I don't believe anything actually fell off the back of a lorry because my grandparents – it rubbed off on my Dad – were scrupulously law-abiding. Dad, as an adult more extravagant – I should probably say generous – and not always smart with money might have chafed against this frugal regime while he was growing up. I remember him telling me how he once tried to save up the money he was earning as a paper-boy to buy himself a bicycle. He tried to keep it quiet from the rest of the family but one day his mother found him in the bedroom with all the coins spread out, counting up to see if he had enough for the bike. 'Where did you get all that money?' she demanded. Dad explained how he had earned it. 'Well you need a new coat,' she replied, and scooped up all his cash.

He never got his bicycle. But he did remember, from a time when he was a bit smaller, a much-loved pedal car. His Peddly-Motor, he called it. It was red and like all such vehicles it had no brakes. If he was careering down the pavement and he had to stop, he would stick his arm out and grab a lamp-post. Such are the fragments of childhood memory, like the name of Charlie Grout. Charlie came up again and again in his reminiscences, a special friend. He and Dad were, it seems, inseparable. I never asked Dad who Charlie was, where he lived, what he did when he grew up. It was only through Dad's brother Ron that I learned, much later, that little Charlie wasn't just a friend but a cousin who lived with the family because he had been unofficially 'adopted'. For reasons never discussed and still unknown. With nine kids already under the same roof, it didn't seem to matter if they squeezed in one more.

Dad used to tell me, when I was young, that education and hard work were the routes to success in life and I'm pretty sure I embraced the ethos very early on. I can recall memories of infants' school, learning to read and write and do arithmetic and never questioning the value of all that graft with a stubby pencil, neatly forming the letters and numbers against the lines on the page. True, the letters and words always behaved themselves better than the numbers, but in my unformed brain I recognised that it was all valuable, all important. What intrigues me now is how Dad, a man from a working class family whose own parents had had the minimum of formal education came to have such enthusiasm for his own kids' schooling.

I found a letter, typed on flimsy paper from the Borough of Bexley Electricity Department and dated 20th June 1947. It is a reference, certifying that up to that date and excluding time in His Majesty's forces, Dad had worked for the department since the 30th December 1935. The letter is signed by W. Wicks, Borough Electrical Engineer, who described Dad as follows:

'Mr. Bull is a young man of excellent character, he is conscientious in his work, is a good workman and is absolutely dependable in every respect. While I shall be sorry to lose his services I wish him every success in his efforts to improve his position and hope that in later years I hear that he has made the progress he deserves.'

Reading that I feel pride – that was my Dad Mr Wicks was writing about – and gratitude that in those days an employer had the inclination and the time to put down on paper something so personal. I summon Mr Wicks to my imagination (with waistcoat and watch-chain, for a bit of colour) dictating the letter to his personal secretary. Perhaps they exchanged a few words, opinions, about young Mr Bull who was taking himself off with his wife and baby to a new life overseas. Similar letters follow, spanning the fifties, sixties and seventies, and they carry the same picture of Dad's dependability, conscientiousness, and sobriety. What sets this letter apart from the others is that first date: 30th December 1935. That was three days before Dad's 14th birthday and it was the day he was taken on, according to the letter, as a Showroom Lad.

I keep asking myself what a fourteen-year-old boy is qualified to do, to justify a weekly wage, in an electrical showroom. Perhaps he made tea and swept the floors and polished those shiny electrical appliances for the benefit of increasingly well-heeled consumers. Dad's entry into the world of work coincided with a time of growth and relative prosperity in Britain, especially in the south of England. The Great Depression was over and along with rising employment thousands of new homes – with electricity - were being built in towns and suburbs all over the south-east of the country. Steady wages and low interest rates meant that a Baby Belling electric cooker or a Hoover Junior vacuum cleaner could be taken away on hire purchase and shown off in the sparkling new semi in Acacia Avenue.

Young Jack Bull – I'm guessing that at that age he still hung on to the family nickname – must have found it all pretty glamorous. I don't know how many of the customers noticed the skinny boy with the big ears, or if he was even allowed to make his presence known, let alone actually talk to the clientele, but he would still have felt part of their grown-up world, as fast-changing and shiny as the products on the showroom floor. He wasn't to know that the surge of prosperity was fuelled in part by the government spending like crazy to re-arm against Germany, but he would have been starting to read the papers and listening to the grown-ups talking about Mussolini marching into Abyssinia, about the Olympic Games in Hitler's Berlin, and by the end of his first year in the job, the abdication of Edward VIII.

Dad's education may have been rudimentary, but as an adult he was always eager to learn and had a strong interest in current affairs. When I was about ten or eleven years old I went on a journey with him in our family car and the conversation somehow came around to the Soviet Union. This would have been in 1968 or 1969. 'I'd rather be dead than live in a communist country,' said Dad. I remember the shock of hearing it; while I had a vague inkling that the Russians were wicked while the Americans were our friends I couldn't imagine that anywhere could be so bad, that it would be better to be dead. But he meant it. Dad was never blatantly right-wing; rather he was firmly antileft. He told me how as a young paper-boy (whether this was before Showroom Lad or a job on the side, I don't know), he had to deliver the Daily Worker to one particular house on his round, just one copy amongst all the Daily Expresses and News Chronicles. Because he knew it was a nasty communist paper, he devised a technique of re-folding the pages before he pushed the paper through the customer's letter-box, so that it would arrive on the hall-way floor in a tangled and inconvenient heap. Thereby my short-trousered father did his bit to counter the Red Threat and sacrificed any chance of a tip at Christmas.

This takes us a long way from the topic of education. Dad wasn't unusual leaving school at the age of fourteen, the minimum legal age at that time. In his family staying on at school to gain formal qualifications would have been out of the question. With nine surviving children from a family of ten – and not counting the mysterious Charlie Grout - each one had to pay their way as soon as they were able. Dad once told me that his twin sisters Daisy and Violet showed academic promise and had been offered places at a grammar school, but their father forbade them to take up the offer and like their brothers and sisters they started work at fourteen. Incidentally, I recently repeated this version of events to Daisy, now in her nineties, and she denied it was true, but it was still a fact that she went on to have a successful career in management. In any event, instead of the School Certificate and whatever doors that might have opened, teen-aged Daisy and Violet followed the example of their mother and became domestic servants. I wonder now how much of their parents' opposition to educational betterment was rooted in genuine economic need. Was it simply a case of wanting your offspring to 'know their place' in what was then a deeply class-ridden society?

I own one photograph of my paternal grandfather, a man with a sour face in a flat cap. He was actually born a

Dennis, not a Bull, and had been adopted by his widowed mother's second husband, so I dare say he had had his own trials along the way. My Dad never had a single word to say in his favour, even on the day he heard that he had died. I remember it clearly. It was December 1971 - we were in Zambia at the time – and Dad received the news by telegram. I was home for the Christmas holidays from my boarding school in England and I was playing in the garden when Dad came out of the house to tell me that Grandad Bull had passed away. I had no idea what I was supposed to say; it was the first time that death had entered my life. I think I mumbled something about how I was sorry for Dad, and he simply said, dry-eyed, 'It's alright, I wasn't close to him anyway', and walked back into the house.

***

Last year I spent a weekend with Dad's two surviving siblings. Auntie Daisy is ninety-three, the twin to Violet and a near-contemporary of Dad's within the twenty-year span of family births. Daisy was only a few years younger than Dad and in his lifetime he always talked of her as one of the special ones. My uncle Ron is the other half of the remnant pair and at the age of eighty-three (he looks much younger) very much the baby of the family. By the time Ron was old enough to have any memories of Dad, Dad was almost an adult. Ron and his wife Cathy preside over a brood of their own and have recently been given their first great-grand-daughter.

Having seen neither Daisy nor Ron for nearly twenty years, and with only intermittent contact before that, there was a lot of catching up to do. I couldn't really explain why we had let the family bonds stretch so thin. Because I had grown up in Africa and then in adult life lived in different parts of England, and latterly abroad, I suppose the only excuse to get together had been the occasional family funeral. I never knew my cousins (I have twenty of them,

I've found, on Dad's side of the family) and I never went to any of their weddings or their kid's christenings. In any case quite a few of them live in Australia. I guess it might have been different if Dad hadn't been the first among his brothers and sisters to die or if Mum had survived him. If they had lived longer either or both of them would have joined in with the odd family event and kept us all a bit more connected. Without them steering the ship I've drifted off, untethered.

Stewart (and Tony, when he was alive) have made a bit more effort over the years but for the most part the contact has been with Mum's side of the family where we have two cousins, close in age to Tony and Stewart. As the baby of our own family trio perhaps I've just jogged along in a little world of my own and left all this extended family stuff to the grown-ups. Selfish, you could say, and I'd probably try to defend myself by saying that nobody would be much interested in what I'm doing anyway, so why bother?

When Jude and I first arrived at Ron and Cathy's house in Bexley I made some comment over the tea and biscuits and photo albums about spending much of my life overseas and how that had made it hard to keep in touch. Cathy, almost straight-faced, said that they'd thought that perhaps I was simply too stuck-up to want to know them. If it wasn't for the Irish twinkle that went with the remark, and the warmth and love and welcoming-in I received from Cathy and Ron, the words might have stung. But it got me thinking. If families can be such a support and refuge, why had I not made the effort to cling on to this ready-made network of uncles and aunts and cousins when I lost my own Dad and Mum so long ago? Stewart might explain it by saying I had always been a loner, the odd one. Perhaps he would be right.

Dad, as his brother and sister remembered him, was almost my complete opposite. Time and again Daisy or Ron would say that their Jack was the one-off among all the brothers and sisters, the one with ambition. Outgoing and warm and kind and funny. Optimistic. He wanted a wider world and he was prepared to take chances to find it. All this was anathema to his father. The head of the family had been born in 1888, in an era that already looked prehistoric to his offspring growing up in the 1930s and 1940s. His childhood had seen few comforts and no safety net so perhaps we shouldn't be surprised that security, of employment, of home, was his overriding concern. From his perspective, any attempt to better yourself, to 'get on', represented the one thing he always tried to avoid - risk. Ron told me about a time in the 1950's when he decided to leave his position at the London Electricity Board and look for something better. His father was devastated, and angry. In the mind of a man who grew up in the shadow of the workhouse, why would anyone let go a steady, secure job?

In today's language we might say he was managing expectations. Unable to imagine himself rising beyond the level of an underpaid warehouseman, he feared that his children would get hopes beyond the possible, take unnecessary chances and suffer disappointment and ruin. He made that clear to my Dad once when he told him 'you'll never own a motor car. ' Dad never forgot that conversation and it made him determined to own that forbidden motor as soon as he could afford it. But Dad's dreams went further, in directions that the old man would never have expected.

When I asked Dad's siblings about their father, they were a little more charitable about him than Dad ever was. Uncle Ron, thirteen years Dad's junior, remembers their father as a man of narrow outlook, almost illiterate, but utterly devoted to his wife and family. When I asked Ron about his own relationship with his father, he told me that he simply used to feel frustrated seeing his Dad work so hard for so little and for so long – an unimaginable continuum of nearly six decades - for a single employer.

Auntie Daisy, closer in age to my Dad, took a similar view, acknowledging that while her mother was the 'educated one', her father was 'a limited man'. I think this limitation of outlook, the stolid lack of imagination and ambition, would have been the source of Dad's antipathy towards him.

My own memories of Grandad Bull come from intermittent childhood visits to my grandparents' house in the sixties and early seventies. He was permanently installed in an armchair next to the fireplace while his wife, warm, loving Nan Bull was in a state of constant busy-ness, making tea and serving meals and generally making sure everyone was looked after. Her energy and devotion to her family after producing ten children was humbling, although I didn't appreciate it at the time. Her husband wasn't infirm, by the way. I think he just couldn't be bothered to get out of his armchair. Why would you, when your wife has waited on you hand and foot for half a century? Apparently he believed that he had already made a major contribution to family life, by fathering ten kids. This was his point of pride. I once asked Dad why his parents had had so many children; they weren't Roman Catholics and while larger families were more common in their day, most couples were prepared to stop at three or four. Dad's explanation was straightforward. 'I think they were just over-sexed, ' he said.

TWO

By the time Dad was in his late teens the British cinema-building boom was in full swing and hundreds of modern picture houses were appearing in town centres all over the country. Film programmes were shown almost continuously and many people visited the cinema two or three times a week. It was glamourous escapism. The cinema companies, ABC, Gaumont and Odeon knew what they were doing, drawing in the crowds with vast art-deco palaces that did more than just show you a film. They gave you an experience. Plush seats and dim lights, pretty usherettes in neat uniforms and boys with trays selling chocolate and cigarettes. Ice cream and Saturday clubs for the children.

And live entertainment. This was what caught Dad's eye as a teenage regular at the two thousand seater Bexleyheath Regal. They began to run talent shows – the 1930s equivalent of the X Factor – and Dad fancied his chances. He decided to pitch himself against the other hopefuls, an assortment of singers, jugglers, conjurers and acrobats. He put together a routine which included impersonations of Churchill and Hitler and Mussolini – standard fare for the day - but the *piece de resistance* was a lingeringly drawn-out portrayal of a lady undressing for the bath. Uncle Ron remembers seeing his big brother's antics on the stage; their mother had taken him when he was about seven, but their father didn't go.

The night little Ron had seen his brother miming the lady sliding off her stockings and wriggling out of her corset, the judges gave Dad second place in the competition. According to Dad, that was only part of the journey. There were more shows and some sort of knock-out leading to a final winner being announced at the end of a season. He may have had to perform at other cinemas, but no-one can remember. The important detail is that Dad eventually won the competition. He was on the road to stardom and he wasn't yet twenty.

This is where his father comes back into the picture. He hadn't made the effort to go and see his son perform, to hear the laughter and applause of two thousand people, but that didn't stop him having an opinion. When Dad told his parents that the prize for winning the competition was a contract as the paid warm-up act for one of the big dance bands, touring the seaside resorts for a summer season, his father didn't hesitate to put his foot down. Never mind that Dad would be paid four or five times what he was earning as an electrician. No son of his was going to do something as stupid as to give up a solid job as a tradesman for a summer's work as an entertainer. He forbade it, and killed the dream. Dad was an obedient son so he accepted the ruling and got on with his life. The war was already under way and it wasn't long before he was old enough to join up. He wanted to do his bit – his stage impressions of the dictators weren't going to defeat fascism – but he wasn't too keen to join the Poor Bloody Infantry. So Dad, along with a like-minded work-mate presented himself at the recruiting office for the Royal Navy. The only snag was that thousands of other young men were equally eager to avoid land-based combat, and by 1942 the senior service was over-subscribed. Dad was refused but his friend (I believe his name was Jim Mundy) was accepted, thanks to an arbitrary policy which gave preference to men who already had a relative in the navy. Within a year Jim was dead. He was a stoker aboard the destroyer HMS Harvester when it was torpedoed in the North Atlantic by the German submarine U-432.

Dad was offered the option to join the Royal Marines so he signed up and stayed in uniform for four years. He told me that it was the best thing that he could have done. He loved the life because it took him away from the strictures of family and showed him the world. At first, seeing the world meant getting away from Bexleyheath and mixing for the first time with men from other parts of the UK. He loved that, the novelty of it. Basic training was in Lympstone in Devon, where the Marines still train their recruits today. It took about six weeks, Dad's introduction to Khaki Green Uniform No.4, the legendary drill sergeant ('I am your mother, your father, and the biggest bastard you will ever meet '), spit-and-polish and the Lee Enfield .303 rifle. Along with thousands of other young men he passed through the sausage machine, enduring route marches and obstacle courses with progressively heavier burdens of kit – over ninety pounds by the end of training, according to some accounts – and a multitude of novel demands which, seemingly, he took in his stride.

After basic training he was posted to HMS Gosling, not a real ship but a Royal Navy 'stone frigate', a shore establishment near Risley, roughly mid-way between Liverpool and Manchester. It was the first time Dad had been north of Watford. Gosling was newly established. It had been set up primarily to train technicians for the Fleet Air Arm but it also hosted the training of Royal Marines for the Royal Naval Air Station Defence Force. It was at Gosling that Dad was trained as an armourer, a trade he was to return to in Africa twelve years later. I don't know if he was ever earmarked for the defence of air stations; after completing his examinations as an armourer he was posted to the Second Mobile Naval Base Defence Organisation – MNBDO II. Although Dad never mentioned this outfit (I only read it in his service record) I found that it was an important component of the Royal Marines – 'the Corps' – during the Second World War. An MNBDO comprised units with a variety of skills, weapons and equipment ostensibly tasked with the defence of a mobile naval base established by the Royal Navy. This meant defence from the land, sea and air and required, according to the needs of the operation, anti-aircraft gunners, searchlight units and artillery as well as men and hardware capable of specialised beach operations. At times MNBDO units even included RAF radar systems and barrage balloons under their command.

The MNBDOs started small. The first unit, MNBDO I, was formed just after the outbreak of war. It comprised only around 2,000 men, the numbers doubling within months through the recruitment of 'Hostilities Only' officers and marines. These were the HO's, men like Dad who had arrived from all walks of life and in the eyes of the 'regulars' not quite the real thing. One of Dad's Sergeant-Majors reserved his favourite catch-phrase for them: 'You HO's give me the shits'. As the war progressed MNBDO I units found themselves shifted progressively eastward, serving in Crete, Egypt and Ceylon. Meanwhile MNBDO II was formed by a small rump from MNBDO I and topped up with several thousand more HO's. In the year Dad enlisted, 1942, many MNBDO II units were deployed for the coastal defence of England, but by the end of that year, just as Dad was graduating from HMS Gosling, the organisation was making ready for operations overseas.

Because we know the history we find it almost impossible, over seventy-five years later, to imagine the sense of unknowing experienced by those men who were launched beyond home shores by the momentum of the war. They didn't know where they were going and perhaps those who sent them didn't always know the final destination. Almost none of them had ever been abroad. In that icy January of 1943, when he lugged his kit up the gangway of a troopship in Liverpool, Dad could not have known that by the middle of summer he would be stepping off a landing craft into the warm waters of a Mediterranean beach with bullets and shells flying over his head. Nor would he have been sure that he would see England again, or even his next birthday.

On the ship, of course, rumour and speculation abounded. Carrying tropical kit meant Africa, or the Middle East. Maybe Greece or Italy, or somewhere farther afield. It could even mean fighting the Japanese. The men could be grateful to the Japs, in a way. Thanks to them, thanks to Pearl Harbor, the Americans were now firmly in the game and the odds were shifting in Britain's favour. But closer to home the U-boats were still at large and taking their toll on allied shipping. Dad and his comrades might have been torpedoed and drowned long before they faced an enemy bullet.

Faced with such a prospect a lot of men like Dad, if they had a sweetheart at home, chose to marry her before they sailed. There were many reasons for this which must include the desire to consummate their love before possibly having their young lives cut short. It was also practical economics; if you were killed in service your widow would receive a pension. I never asked Mum or Dad their motives. They married in a narrow window of opportunity on Boxing Day 1942, just a week or so before Dad shipped out. It was a classic austerity wedding, without a long white gown (clothing ration) or a three-tier cake (sugar ration). My uncle Kim, Mum's brother-in-law offered to do the photographs but according to family folklore he forgot to put a film in his camera.

The girl Dad married was Doreen Stewart, a hairdresser from Woolwich. They had met on a blind date when Dad wasn't yet in uniform and you can still see their first meeting place, the clock tower on Bexleyheath Broadway, although it is now dwarfed by a shopping mall. Doreen, my Mum, came from an outwardly respectable lower middle class family. She was the youngest of three sisters – a little boy, Tommy, had died before Mum was born – and her Scottish father had been a career soldier who had run away from home and lied about his age to join up. He served in India, spent four years in France with the Royal Field Artillery and survived a shrapnel wound at the battle of Mons.

After leaving the service he became a junior civil servant; my Mum remembers him commuting daily into Whitehall with a rolled umbrella under his arm and his shoes shining like a mirror. He was a joker – when Mum was too young to know better she believed his stories about buying bottles of bread – and something of a philanderer. His favourite expression when he spied a tall and attractive woman was 'she's got legs right up to her doo-dah'. He never returned to his native Scotland but always insisted, when out for a walk with his little daughters, that any thistles they might meet along the way had to be saluted. When war came in 1939 the former Warrant Officer tried to re-enlist in the army, only to be disappointed when they told him he was too old.

I never knew Grandad Stewart because he died of a heart attack at the age of sixty-five, not long after my brother Tony was born. His wife, our Nana Stewart, I met only a handful of times when I was small and she made no particular impression on me apart from the few shillings she gave me to buy sweets. The occasional remark picked up from Mum makes me think that Nana Stewart rather looked down on Dad's family and in return I know they didn't think much of her. Mum was devoted to her.

In 1942, war or no war, you had to have your parents' permission to get married if you were under twenty-one. Mum was only nineteen but as far as I know her parents didn't raise any objections, even if Mrs Stewart thought that her daughter could have done better. Dad's father, on the other hand, made it clear that Jack was too young to marry and initially refused his permission. Somehow, in the end, it all got sorted out. They married a week before Dad's twenty-first birthday and his father refused to attend the ceremony.

In the spring of 1940, before Mum met Dad, her family evacuated her and her middle sister to the home of a relative in Edinburgh to escape the bombing of London. Mum had to give up hairdressing and briefly worked as a cinema usherette. This coincided with the release of Walt Disney's Pinocchio, a film which Mum came to know in intimate detail. Before long they returned home to Woolwich and Mum joined the thousands of women being pulled into 'war work'. In Mum's case this meant a position in a factory manufacturing radio equipment for the armed services. As a youngster with sharp eyes and a steady hand she was recruited to execute the intricate soldering of electronic valves, the heart of radio technology in the days before the invention of the transistor. The standard of her workmanship was recognised and she was moved into a special section producing the 'peanut valve', a tiny component for installation in what were then considered 'lightweight' radios. I imagine the work required immense concentration and stamina but I think Mum enjoyed it. There was camaraderie in the place and the daily routine was broken up from time to time by morale-lifting talks from the troops.

One of the officers brought in to visit the factory had just returned from fighting the Japanese in Burma. His unit had been on a narrow and treacherous mountain trail, leading a string of donkeys laden with stores, weapons and other equipment including – you've guessed it – field radios produced by that very same factory. One of the donkeys, the story went, missed its footing on the stony escarpment and tumbled down the cliff, falling hundreds of feet to the valley floor. 'Well ladies,' said the officer, 'we made our way down and we eventually found that donkey. Of course the poor beast was dead. But we retrieved the radio off his back and do you know what? It was working perfectly, good as new.'

Such was the novelty of war work. Mum carried on with it after she married and learned to adjust to her new status as a service wife with a man overseas. Married or not, she was still an attractive young woman and inevitably there were admirers. Being wartime, each month there seemed to be more and more soldiers, sailors and airmen. They came from all over the country and increasingly from abroad, creatures from exotic places like Melbourne or Cincinnati or Toronto. There was something of the film-star about some of them. One who wandered into Mum's orbit was a Canadian airman whose name I can't remember (Eddie? Danny?). She never explained to me how he appeared in her life, but he started to become a regular caller at the house where Mum and her sister still lived with their parents. My grandmother encouraged him, perhaps judging that he was a better catch than Dad and calculating that he would be worth hanging on to in case her daughter's husband didn't come home. Mum said that she argued with her mother about it, reminding her that she was already married, and eventually the young Canadian, who Mum remembered with some fondness, drifted away.

Meanwhile, Dad was probably unaware of the goings-on at home. His troop ship took him south, to Cape Town, a long way from the action. He was allowed time ashore there, his first step onto foreign soil. When he talked about the place he only recounted one specific memory. He recalled the image of a city park, where dozens of squirrels had been individually garroted and were hanging, dead, from the branches of trees. The killing spree had been carried out by a crowd of drunken Australian soldiers, for fun. After Cape Town the ship continued anti-clockwise around Africa, through the Red Sea and the Suez Canal, and the Marines were deposited in Alexandria. Here the serious training began; preparation for beach landings on foreign soil, real operations facing a real enemy.

For many years we kept a precious artefact from Dad's spell in Egypt, but for now it is lost; perhaps one day it will show up in somebody's attic. It is an Airgraph, an item roughly the size of a postcard with a glossy finish like a photograph. Airgraphs were a wartime invention taken up when the authorities realised that they could make the carriage of mail by air more efficient by photographing the letters and recording them on micro-film. The rolls of film, weighing fifty times less than the original documents, would be flown home to the UK or another location with suitable facilities where the letters were printed off on photographic paper then sent on by domestic mail. Before long the format evolved and senders could buy pre-printed cards to write their messages on. Many of these were amateur jobs and, like the one Dad sent to Mum in the Spring of 1943, carried a simple drawing to convey the flavour of the place of origin. The Airgraph which Mum received and cherished for all those years carried a simple message of love scribbled above an image of a camel with a palm tree in the background. Underneath Dad wrote 'The magic east – it stinks '. So without offending the censors, Mum was informed that her husband was somewhere in the Middle East and that he hadn't forgotten her. Where he was exactly, doing what, she obviously had no idea. But at least for the time being she knew he was safe.

After several weeks of training in Alexandria the Marine units were transported west to Malta which was becoming the hub for an enormous invasion force. At what stage the troops were told that they would invade Sicily I don't know. After their defeat in North Africa the Germans were expecting the Allies to launch an offensive into southern Europe. A complex deception operation was executed to lead the Axis powers to expect an attack on Greece, which included the deployment of decoy troop divisions in Syria, a fictitious headquarters in Egypt and, famously, Operation Mincemeat. Mincemeat involved depositing the dead body of a homeless man, dressed as a Royal Marines officer, off the coast of Spain. He was carrying a briefcase, attached to his belt, containing forged documents which hinted that the assault targets could be Greece, Sardinia or Corsica. As hoped, the supposedly neutral Spanish passed the information to their Nazi friends and it is believed that Hitler made major changes to troop deployments as result of the false information. Thousands of allied lives may have been saved; certainly the invasion of Sicily was a success and cost far fewer losses in men and ships than the planners had expected.

For western Europeans and North Americans the crowning achievement of World War Two is remembered as the Normandy landings, while the Sicily campaign – Operation Husky - is either unknown or viewed as a side-show to the main event. But Husky was an enormous undertaking and arguably involved more men landing over a wider front than the better-know Operation Overlord. Over 3,000 ships, 4,000 aircraft and 150,000 men – mostly British, American and Canadian – took part on the allied side on the morning of the invasion, the 10th of July 1943. The enemy they faced comprised a quarter of a million Axis soldiers, about a third of them German, all nominally under Italian command.

During thirty-eight days of fighting the allied forces under the command of General Eisenhower suffered 25,000 casualties as they drove the Italians to surrender and the Germans to a mass retreat to the Italian mainland. Within such a grand event, a turning point in the most devastating war in human history, it pains me that I know so little about the part my Dad played. We can only speculate, imagining him waiting out the hours of darkness in his landing craft before his unit hit the beach near Augusta. What were those first moments like, facing the enemy? How close did he get to taking a bullet; how many around him fell? He never shared any specifics.

There were a handful of anecdotes but few of them reflected the reality of armed combat. Before the assault Dad remembered suffering from dysentery in Malta, a trial he sat out for a day or two on a cliff-top latrine with a view over a memorably picturesque coastline. He never talked about the actual day of the beach landing in Sicily but he recalled the sight and smell of a burned-out Sherman tank full of decaying American corpses. Some of his own friends lost their lives during the campaign. When the fighting was over there was an acquaintance with a pretty Italian farm girl – no other details given – and the informal requisitioning of a tired old horse which Dad claimed to have ridden bareback, quite a feat for an electrician from Bexleyheath. He also claimed to have shot down a Heinkel bomber with an Oerlikon anti-aircraft gun. It sounds unlikely as Dad was not a gunner but an armourer, but we will never know. The last big event before Dad left Sicily was the celebration of Christmas, 1943. By tradition Marine units would arrange a role-swap on Christmas day, with the Commanding Officer switching positions (and uniforms) with a man from the ranks. Marine Bull, not unused to treading the boards, was chosen to be the senior officer for the day and apparently he played the part swaggeringly well.

The following month Dad was on his way home.

THREE

Dad was proud to have been part of a unit that had served overseas and he told me that when he and his buddies returned home early in 1944 they were eager to be kept together and fight again as part of the long-awaited Second Front. This came to fruition with the Normandy landings in June of that year, but the young marines were to be disappointed; their unit was never sent to France, or into any of the European campaigns which led to victory over Germany on the eighth of May 1945. In the months before D-Day Dad was stationed back at Lympstone, where he had completed basic training, and Mum took lodgings in a cottage nearby. She remembered enduring cat-calls and wolf-whistles from the truckloads of American soldiers who passed by – she was embarrassed to be seen at the side of the road collecting water from a hand-pump – and wondered in later years how many of those boys had died on the French beaches that summer.

We have all seen the images and newsreels from VE Day. Servicemen jitterbug with grinning girls in Trafalgar Square. The war-tired of Britain frolic in fountains, wave flags, get drunk. They form conga lines, they indulge in the Hokey Cokey and they crowd around Buckingham Palace to see the King and Queen and Mr Churchill waving from the balcony. As far as I know my Mum and Dad didn't jitterbug that day; they never mentioned it, anyway. They probably weren't even together on the day of celebration, as Dad still had a year to go before his de-mobilisation from the Marines. He wouldn't have known that at the time; a lot of the talk in the ranks during that summer was about how long the bloody Japs were going to keep fighting and whether this regiment or ship or squadron would be shipped out to the Far East to help the Yanks finish the job. It could have gone on for years. Meanwhile Dad languished in the Royal Marine depots in Deal and Chatham, waiting for something to happen. He smoked cigarettes and thought about his future. He had a wife, he had a trade, and he was still only twenty three.

By August the world had learned the words Atom Bomb and the Japanese bowed out of the war. Almost overnight hundreds of thousands of soldiers, sailors and airman across Britain and the Empire had become surplus to requirements. It was a costly burden given the dread state of the nation's finances and the millstone of debt owed to our friends across the Atlantic, yet the military machine would take time to dismantle. Dad had to stay in uniform until May 1946 before he could walk back into the Electricity Department of Bexley Corporation.

He must have taken some home leave during the run-up to de-mobilisation, because my brother Tony was born in March 1946. In adult life Tony, master of the anecdote, liked to tell people that he was conceived on VE Day. The arithmetic doesn't quite work – it would have been an almost elephantine pregnancy – yet I still find it extraordinary that my own brother was born so close to the Second World War. Tony was a tiny, squawking unit in the British baby boom, often lumped in with similar phenomena in countries such as the USA, but in the UK it had quite a different flavour. While returning American servicemen and their young wives were confidently bringing children into a post-war existence of prosperity and fresh food and cheap homes, my Mum and Dad and thousands of their counterparts across Britain were producing offspring more out of youthful optimism than any tangible sense of entering a better world. Nazi bombing had destroyed or left uninhabitable over half a million homes and the surge of house-building was a long way from gaining any momentum.

Like many young couples Mum and Dad and baby had to squeeze in with relatives; in their case it was with Mum's parents in a flat in Barnehurst which they rented above a shop. Their previous home had been blasted by a doodlebug in 1944, when Mum had crouched with her mother and sister in the indoor cage of a Morrison shelter while her father, fresh from an operation for a stomach ulcer, had to lay in bed nearby hoping for the best. They all escaped almost unscathed, the women thanks to Mr Morrison's metal box and, in my grandfather's case, the same lucky star that had watched over him in the trenches during the previous war.

When Dad returned to civilian life rationing – of food, clothing, and petrol - was still in force without much sign of an end and the country was tired, bankrupt and grey. Food, the amount of it, the variety of it, was a gnawing, ever-present concern throughout the war and into the years of recovery. 'I see another sugar boat's been torpedoed' was a routine quip from my Mum's sweet-toothed father when his wife economised on the number of teaspoons she scooped into his tea; sugar rationing had been in force since 1940 and would continue until 1953. And there was a national humiliation that went alongside food rationing, when British people were faced with comparing their meagre lot with the ever-present American servicemen and their bounty of rations.

One day in early 1946 my pregnant Mum paid a visit to Dad at his base at Chatham and he took her out for a turn of the dockyard in a rowing boat. I picture the scene, Dad in his battledress paddling through the oily water and Mum sitting on the hard planks in her maternity outfit. The smell of the sea and the sight of seagulls circling overhead in place of Heinkels and Hurricanes. They approached an anchored US Navy warship and struck up a conversation with the sailors who hailed them from the decks above. The Americans may have been envied, but they were known for their generosity and this particular ship's company showed it by urging Mum and Dad to come back the following day, when the seamen promised they would be able to give them some frozen chickens and various other goodies. The ship's stores had plenty to spare, apparently.

My parents must have been thrilled. Eager to receive their gifts they rowed out again the next day at the agreed time. They located the right anchorage without much trouble, but they found that their American friends had gone. In their place was a ship of the Royal Navy. I doubt that Mum and Dad had been victims of a trick – it was more likely a case of miscommunication or a last-minute change to ship's orders – but the US vessel had definitely sailed overnight. There was a conversation between His Majesty's Ship and the little rowing boat and the deprived British matelots tried begging for some ciggies.

I doubt whether the election of a Labour government in 1945 would have given Dad much cheer. True, he had been able to walk back into his old job in Civvie Street and they just about made ends meet. Mum and Dad were each supported by wider family networks, all pulling together, more or less, and they couldn't be ungrateful that every single one of them, Mum, Dad, their parents and their ten siblings had all survived the war. None of their family members or their spouses were among the half-million from Britain and the Empire who had been killed over the past six years. Those at home had lived through the air raids which dragged Mum from her bed night after night in 1940, a grumbling teen cursing Hitler for stealing her sleep, and again in 1944 when the V1s and V2s arrived.

The boys who had gone overseas returned with all their limbs. Things could have been far, far worse.

But they wanted more. The war had awakened in that generation's young men and women an expectation of getting on, getting ahead, of improving yourself. Of looking forward to a new world and a new order. Class and deference had been, if not swept away, at least diminished. It's what we fought the war for, wasn't it? No more us and them, toffs and workers. There was going to be opportunity, fairer shares, and a return to the prosperity that had been gaining pace back in the late-thirties.

I don't think Dad believed that his brave new dawn was going to come thanks to Mister Attlee and the bolshie trade unions – I'm pretty sure he voted for Churchill's party in the 1945 general election - but he would have been infected by the egalitarian spirit. The problem was that moods and ideas, promises and slogans like Labour for Security and Labour for Homes needed to deliver something pretty sharpish to a young man with a wife and a new baby cramped into a tiny flat with the in-laws. Dad didn't want slogans, he wanted a place to live and a decent meal on the table.

In later years Dad told me that the war was the best thing that ever happened to him. It had shown him a bigger world, a place of rich and wonderful variety. He had seen blue oceans and palm trees and deserts and olive groves. He had experienced the joy of masculine camaraderie, mixing, toiling, battling and laughing with lads from Lancashire mills and West Country farms, with the Welsh and the Irish and the Scots, with Aussies and Canadians and Kiwis and South Africans. He had fought alongside the Yanks and marched past young men, dead or captured, from Italy and Germany. He had seen black people, brown people, and he had felt the sun on his back. The corner of Kent where he had grown up, each year more of a smoky urban sprawl than the land of hops and meadows, would never look or sound or smell the same after South Africa, Egypt or the islands of the Mediterranean. Like many ex-servicemen, Dad shared these experiences with his wife and they considered their options.

Along with hundreds of thousands of others they made up their minds to emigrate. But where to? Having endured the previous winter, one of the fiercest in recent memory, it had to be somewhere warm and sunny; Australia came to mind. But there was a wide range of dominions, colonies and other English-speaking places to choose from. Mum had an elderly spinster aunt – I know nothing more about her – who lived alone in Cape Town and she wrote to say that she was prepared to put them up if they chose to try a new life in South Africa. There were jobs to be had for skilled tradesmen like Dad so letters were written and arrangements were agreed. Before my parents could grasp that it was really happening, they were on their way. On the 27th of January 1948, a wintry Tuesday, Mum and Dad carried little Tony and their sparse collection of luggage onto the Motor Vessel Carnarvon Castle from Southampton.

We can imagine a grim crossing of the Bay of Biscay. According to records from the Met Office it was Britain's wettest January to date and north-west Europe was being buffeted by severe storms. The Carnarvon Castle, no luxury liner, was already over twenty years old and had recently come back into commercial service after wartime operations, first as an armed merchant cruiser and later as a troop ship. After war service the Union Castle Company didn't give the ship's accommodation much of an upgrade so many of the ex-soldiers on board, now travelling with their young wives and kids, may have felt a certain *déjà vu*. Mum, Dad and Tony travelled with 1300 other passengers (over 200 children and babies among them) in a ship that had been designed to carry around 800. Many passengers didn't even have the privacy of a cabin, bunking down instead in same-sex dormitories, troop ship style.

Yet we shouldn't underestimate the shared excitement, the spirit of adventure. Within days of sailing the ship was in warmer, calmer waters. There was a stop in Madeira and a brief trip ashore, where Mum bought broad-brimmed sun-hats for herself and Tony. The hats cost five shillings each; I know that trivial detail because of a scribble in Mum's handwriting on the back of a snapshot, taken on the upper deck of the ship. It shows Dad perched on a white-painted bollard. Or perhaps it's an air vent, I can't tell. He's wearing loose, high-waisted trousers, so baggy they almost look like a sailor's bell-bottoms, with white deck shoes and a short-sleeved shirt. He must have bought the shoes especially for the journey. On his knee he's holding Tony who is not quite two and dressed in dungarees and sandals. Mum stands behind them, her slim legs semi-hidden. Her summer frock has puffed half-length sleeves. She's wearing dark glasses and she and Tony are protected from the sun by the new five-bob hats.

Until this voyage Mum had never been abroad; when she was growing up she might never have imagined she would. She hadn't even been to the Isle of Wight and now she was on her way to the Southern Hemisphere. Young Tony may or may not have been potty-trained – they tried to do it early in those days – but if he wasn't then much of Mum's time on the ship would have been spent in the cramped lower decks washing nappies, the only consolation being the sharing of the experience with other mothers who were literally in the same boat. All unaided, of course, by their husbands who whiled away the time up in the sunlight, smoking and swapping war stories and gathering from one another those precious hints and tips which might help them adjust to life – to get ahead - in Africa.

The journey to Cape Town took around two weeks, just enough time to adjust to the heat of the southern summer which in that part of South Africa reaches its peak in February. Five years earlier Dad had been there as a

Royal Marine on his way to the Mediterranean. For Mum it was all new sights, new sounds and smells and anxieties. The racket of alien tongues, everywhere dominated by the rasping sound of Afrikaans but also - thank God – English. Thousands upon thousands of black faces in a country so obviously run by whites. Meeting, timidly and politely, the mystery English aunt upon whose hospitality their well-being would depend.

Over the past ten years my wife and I have moved ourselves to foreign countries a couple of times. In each case we have done it with a healthy bank-balance and a generous re-location package and we have moved swiftly into a roomy house or apartment in an expat-friendly neighbourhood. For Mum and Dad the move to South Africa carried none of that reassuring ballast. Their savings were modest and they were moving in – again - to a home shared with a relative, this time a complete stranger. Dad started work almost immediately, but they still would have been counting down the days before pay-day at the end of that first week. Not that money worries featured much in their memories of that time, when they reminisced in middle age. They told me about the beauty of the beaches and the white blanket of cloud on top of Table Mountain. I do not know Cape Town, but random names stick in my memory from conversations decades past. Plumstead. Fish Hoek. Simon's Town. Adderley Street, where a new department store of the OK Bazaars chain was being built and Dad was contracted into a team doing the electrical work.

Living with the mystery aunt was short-lived and the parting was uncomfortable, apparently, but I don't know the reason for the falling-out, if indeed there was one. Perhaps an unmarried pensioner set in her ways couldn't cope with a young couple and a boisterous toddler invading her home. A remark written by Mum on the back of a picture of the aunt's house hints at some envy of the old lady's wealth. Anyhow, Mum and Dad had to find another place to live and they ended up in a sort of private lodging house inhabited by a variety of singles, couples and families. Two often-told family tales survive from that period and the first centres on the lodging house itself.

Mum said that from time to time the residents would notice the proprietress of the establishment receiving a visitor of a particular type. These strangers were generally young white women, well-dressed. They would come alone, delivered to the front door in an expensive chauffeur-driven car. They would stay for an hour or sometimes longer, and at the end of their visit the car would come to take them away. After they had gone there would be a strong smell about the place of carbolic soap. I guess that some of the residents knew what was going on but Mum admitted that she was young and naïve and really hadn't a clue. She was also probably too shy to ask, but one day the truth became clear. Without any warning a police car turned up and the landlady was taken away. She was charged with performing illegal abortions, a very serious crime in those days.

The second story was Dad's. After the contract in the department store was finished he was employed in more outdoor work, maintaining and repairing street lighting and neighbourhood electrical supplies. One afternoon he was working in the street in a white residential district when a man rushed out of one of the houses and asked Dad to come with him to witness something going on indoors. Dad followed the man into the house and was led to the living room where a small boy was standing, visibly upset. According to Dad, shortly after he entered the room a large vase which was sitting on the mantelpiece flew across the space in front of him and smashed against a wall. In my memory Dad wasn't susceptible to superstitious notions but when he told that story it was clear that he believed he had witnessed a supernatural phenomenon – he didn't know the word poltergeist – and that it had been caused by the troubled child in the room. He was, the man told Dad, emotionally disturbed because he had just been told that his parents were going to divorce.

I first heard that story over forty years ago and I still don't know what to make of it. The supernatural, the other-worldly never featured much in our family life. Mum and Dad only went to church for christenings, weddings and funerals – even Christmas and Easter didn't warrant a visit – and at home they gave us very little encouragement towards the religious life. True, around the age of seven or eight I was dispatched to Sunday School each week, but I was always unaccompanied. We happened to live conveniently opposite the church and the Sunday School teacher was one of Dad's army buddies by the name of Bill Tweedle. This was in the mid-sixties and I think the church was quite modern, what you might call happy-clappy. I'm guessing that Mr Tweedle had extended the invitation to Mum and Dad to hear the gospel and they had compromised by sending me as the family representative.

I didn't object. I liked Mr Tweedle and it was all good fun with lots of games and quizzes, joining in with the other boys and girls. I suppose some of the Christian message sank in, only to be largely forgotten and then periodically re-kindled at various points in my adult life. Dad's own view was straightforward; he used to say that religion was definitely a good thing as long as you didn't let it take you over. In other words, it belonged in its own compartment. This wasn't quite the way he had been brought up. Nan Bull had been a member of the Baptist church and young Jack and his siblings had been enrolled in the Band of Hope. The Band of Hope was a Christian organisation established in Victorian times alongside the temperance societies, targeted at children and young people to educate them about the dangers of drink. It involved weekly meetings with magic lantern talks and group sing-songs and across the country it became a lively, popular kids' get-together with a peak membership of over three million by the end of the nineteenth century.

Dad would have joined the Band of Hope in the thirties when it was already in decline but that didn't stop him from 'signing the Pledge'. The Pledge was a formal act and pledgers were given a grown-up looking certificate. It was a youngster's voluntary promise to literally sign on the dotted line and abstain from the booze for evermore. Dad signed, took his certificate, and stuck to his pledge, more or less avoiding alcohol for the rest of his life. So whatever the explanation, at least we can be fairly confident that on that distant day in Cape Town he observed the flying vase with a clear head.

1942. The new recruit and the girl he married.
Mum was his first and only girlfriend.

Royal Marines training at Lympstone.
Dad is standing second from left.

Dad's parents, Esther and Harold.

Mum and Dad with Tony, 1947.

FOUR

You can't tell the story of a white man in Africa without talking about the black man, and the relations between the two. Dad, Mum and Tony first set foot on African soil over seventy years ago – three generations, more or less – and white attitudes towards 'people of colour' were different to the norms that are considered acceptable today. I want to say 'fundamentally different', 'unrecognisable', something to convey the gulf between our contemporary views of race and those held by our mid-twentieth century forebears. But I hesitate to overdo the differences.

When Dad started to live and work in South Africa in 1948 the country was only months away from a general election. During the canvassing the incumbent Prime Minister Jan Smuts actually kissed little Tony Bull – I don't think politicians do that anymore – but in spite of the gesture his United Party still lost the election. The winners, the Reunited National Party led by Dr D F Malan, held a key policy at its heart. Here is an extract from their campaign material:

'… *Apartheid, a concept historically derived from the experience of the established White population of the country, and in harmony with such Christian principles as justice and equity. It is a policy which sets itself the task of preserving and safeguarding the racial identity of the White population of the country...* '

The rest, as they say, is history. In a country already heavily segregated, apartheid was entrenched, legalised and defended without compromise for another forty-six years, until 1994 turned South Africa upside down and Nelson Mandela became its first black president. Dad never told me much about the politics of his early time in Africa, except to say that as soon as the National Party – the Nats, as they were known - took power, he saw things quickly shifting in favour of the Afrikaans-speaking whites and against the people like him, the English speakers. The recent history of apartheid may be the account of the oppression of South Africa's blacks and other less-than-white people, but there was another story, about the cultural and political divisions between the white groups.

The most visible divide (perhaps we should say audible, because it manifested itself most obviously through language) was and perhaps still is the separation of most South African whites into two tribes: Afrikaans-speaking descendants of the Dutch settlers who took a foothold in Africa in 1652, and English-speaking folk whose ancestors settled there after the Dutch but who progressively gained the ascendancy. Brutal conflicts, including those the British call the Boer Wars, led to an amalgamation in 1905 of the various territories into the Union of South Africa, effectively a part of the British Empire and by the time of Dad's arrival still part of the Commonwealth where it would stay until 1961.

There were other splits and factions and subdivisions which made the picture less straightforward. If someone was to paint with a very broad brush they might try to show the 'English' whites of that time as more liberal, open to political progress and a bit more comfortable with the development and integration of the blacks. And portray the Afrikaners as more inward-looking, a closed group whose religious convictions underpinned their views on racial purity and belief in a God-given dominion over lesser races. There may be some truth behind these generalisations – there usually is - but the reality, even in 1948, was much more complex. Led by Field Marshal Smuts, the Afrikaner Prime Minister and former Boer War commander, thousands of South Africans, many of them Afrikaners, had only recently fought and died alongside the British in the war against Hitler. As in Britain, young people were grappling with competing ideologies in the post-war era and South Africa even had an active Communist Party. One of its prominent white members, Bram Fischer, came from impeccable Afrikaner stock yet he went on to lead the legal defence of Nelson Mandela. As Dad would say, there was good and bad in all people and he believed that even supporters of apartheid were not without their own core of humanity.

What must have added to the mix was the influx of white immigrants like Dad who didn't arrive with the same mental baggage as the established settlers. Dad wasn't especially political, apart from being rather more 'right' than 'left', but I remember enough about him to know that he carried an instinctive respect for his fellow human being that couldn't be reconciled with the harsher aspects of apartheid. Not that the fate of the black man would have been in the forefront of his concerns. Far from it; Dad needed to earn a living. What he told me about that period was that when he went job-hunting after his first contract ended, the fact that he didn't speak Afrikaans was starting to count against him. It seemed that the pendulum had started to swing against the *Engels* who had dominated the country since the end of the Anglo-Boer Wars.

It is ironic that Dad's next move, to the adjacent territory called South West Africa, was triggered by an offer of work in a town called Gobabis which was then so remote and isolated that almost no one there spoke English. Nor did many of them speak Afrikaans; the white inhabitants were predominantly German stock, descended from settlers of the late nineteenth century who had played their part in acquiring the vast territory for a new German empire, only to lose it all at Versailles when the victors of the First World War divvied up Germany's colonial possessions. By 1949 when Dad arrived in South West Africa it had already been administered by South Africa for twenty years so it was effectively a South African province. As such it was soon to feel the full force of the recent change of government in Pretoria. Some of the tragic consequences echoed forward through the decades and I was able to witness them for myself when I lived in the country – now called Namibia - over sixty years later. But that's another story.

Because Dad isn't here to tell his own tale, and because all he left behind was a disordered selection of photographs, bits of official paraphernalia and a wad of job references, I have had to claim anything which comes my way in order to fill in the gaps. I had a lucky break thanks to my brother Tony. The toddler who sailed to Cape Town with Mum and Dad in 1947 had his life cut short in 1999 but a few years before his death he made up his mind to write down a description of his own life so far. The hand-written manuscript only amounts to about a dozen pages – his story never made it beyond the age of eighteen – but it gives the fullest account I have of our family's life during the years which straddle the 1950's. With Tony being twelve years older than me his recollections span, conveniently, the years which pre-date my own.

It is through Tony's handwriting - always far tidier than mine - that I read of his own earliest memories. He remembered his third birthday in Cape Town and receiving a present: a small cardboard suitcase containing (he doesn't say 'full of') chocolate raisins. For the life that was to come a suitcase was a prescient gift. Not long after that birthday Tony and Mum, who was pregnant once more, sailed back to England while Dad headed overland to work unaccompanied in Gobabis. I never knew why Mum and Tony didn't go with him but I guess it was because Mum might have struggled in such a dry and alien place. It wouldn't compare with cosmopolitan Cape Town and its mellow maritime climate.

In 2014 my wife Jude and I visited Gobabis. It now sits on a well-kept highway which stretches across Namibia's vast landscape from the capital Windhoek into western Botswana. It is in the centre of arid cattle-farming country, much as it was back in 1949, and while the town must have grown and modernised over the years it is still a small and remote place where you can hear German spoken in the bars and cafés. When we made our visit I didn't see anyone who looked anywhere near Dad's age but I kept hoping I would bump into some ancient woman or man who might remember the young Englishman who came to fix up the town with electricity. That was why he was there; a generator was being installed and they needed someone to wire up the town.

I've mentioned that Dad hung on to a collection of job-related documents but the one which I can't find anywhere was a paper he wrote in the sixties about bringing the miracle of electricity to Gobabis. I remember reading it as a child and it breaks my heart that we've lost it. Dad was only twenty-seven when he embarked on the project and he got the job done in about eight months. It stretched his skills beyond anything he had attempted before - it was the first time he had had to manage a labour force, organise supplies and logistics and keep everything within a budget – and it was all achieved by working with people, black and white, who didn't speak his language.

While we were driving around the dusty streets of Gobabis I tried to picture Dad there. What did he do with his time, when he wasn't working? He didn't drink much; nor did he read a great deal. As far as I know he didn't do any sport and I doubt there was much to be had in those days, unless by 'sport' you mean going out to the bush to shoot something for your dinner. I do remember him mentioning an older German man who befriended him and I think they played a regular game of chess, handy for people with no common language. He would have got through a lot of cigarettes and filled his evenings writing letters home to Mum, and to his own mother, and waited for the replies to arrive with the frustrations of time-lag and overlap which people put up with in the days before email and FaceTime. You had to get used to the fact that you might write a piece of news on a Monday and then receive a letter on Tuesday asking you a question which you wish you could have answered yesterday and... so it went on. Of course you could get round all that if you used the almost instantaneous magic of the telegram, but it was expensive, and telephone calls were even dearer. When Dad finished his project in Gobabis the town council rewarded him with two gifts: a wristwatch and a ten-minute phone call home. That call to my Mum cost the council ten pounds, around two hundred in today's money.

Apparently the Gobabis council had asked Dad to stay on and look after their newly electrified town, but he decided to head home to his family. For the past eight months Mum and Tony had been living at number 82 Standard Road, the small house in Bexleyheath where Dad was born, and half-way through that time Mum had given birth to my brother Stewart. At the time Nan and Grandad Bull still had their youngest son, my uncle Ron living at home. Ron was an adult with his own room so Mum and the kids must have been piled together; I don't remember the house having more than three bedrooms. An indoor lavatory was tagged on downstairs at the back of the kitchen. Those were the arrangements I can remember from the early sixties and even then there was still no bathroom.

Mum and Tony took the train down to Southampton to meet Dad off the ship, leaving baby Stewart with his grandmother. Mum may or may not have been overjoyed to see her beloved husband but none of the emotion of the reunion was ever recounted in family tales from that time. Mum only remembered her embarrassment – and the sideways looks of the other occupants of the railway compartment – when Tony, who had been bursting to make the announcement ever since leaving home, told his father 'Daddy, you'll never guess – I've got a baby brother! '

In her younger days Mum was easily embarrassed. Anything to do with reproduction (human or animal) or other unseemly bodily functions was pretty much taboo as a topic of conversation, at least *devant les enfants*. Yet, as she settled into her later years she started to relax a bit and even shared the odd joke against herself. She told me about a time in the late sixties when the family was back in Africa (I'm jumping ahead here – there is a lot more to-ing and fro-ing to come) and we lived in a house with a septic tank in the back garden. The house belonged to the government and the local Public Works Department, the PWD, was responsible for emptying the tank at prescribed intervals. One day, Mum said, the kind of smell you associate with such arrangements began to permeate the house with some force and she went out to see what was going on. The tank was overflowing, and the contents spreading across the lawn. The PWD was called and two African operatives arrived to investigate. Mum stood by, close enough to monitor the proceedings but far enough removed to keep her feet dry. Tools were retrieved from the PWD truck and various manholes and covers were removed. You might think it was a simple matter of emptying the tank – perhaps it had been delayed beyond its usual schedule – but apparently not. The body language and the whisperings between the specialists suggested that the problem was more technical.

After much stick-poking and peering and head-shaking the operative-in-chief turned to my mother and announced his diagnosis.

'Too much shit'.

Mum, ever sensitive to personal criticism, glared back and said 'Well don't look at me! '

***

Back to 1950. Mum and Dad, Tony and Stewart were reunited. They continued to stay at 82 Standard Road and Dad returned to work. Things had moved on during his two-and-a-half years abroad and now he was employed by the London Electricity Board – the LEB - not the Bexley Corporation, thanks to the Labour government's mass nationalisation and amalgamation of dozens of private and municipal electricity suppliers. That government was still in power in 1950 and it had carried out the transformative interventions in welfare, health care and so on which make some of us moist-eyed and nostalgic today. Dad would have had his own opinions about all that and more than likely he used his vote in the February election to try and bring back the Conservatives under Churchill. Without success, on that occasion, but the Labour Party took a hammering. Their majority was almost wiped out and in a further election the following year the electorate terminated, for the time being, its love affair with socialism.

Work-wise, there was a change of direction for Dad. Rather than slipping back into his old routine as an electrician, repairing street lights or wiring up houses, he was placed in the showroom. His title was Service Centre Assistant. I asked my uncle Ron, who also worked for the LEB at the time, whether that would have been a come-down, shifting from skilled technical work to the sales floor. Quite the opposite, explained Ron. The showroom men in their suits and ties, or at least some of them, rather looked down on their colleagues with overalls and toolboxes. They spent their days in the warm and dry and kept their fingernails clean. But, I asked, why would they have chosen Dad for a job like that? Ron smiled. 'You knew your Dad. He had the gift of the gab. He was perfect for it. '

When you are in your twenties you are changing and developing at a rate that slows down in later years. In 1950 Dad would not have been the man he was when he left the country in 1947. And that place, Britain, had changed while his back was turned. The welfare state and the widespread nationalisations were more than simple outputs of a left-leaning government, to be argued over between advocates of competing economic models. The new institutional structures – in fact not entirely new, given that some of the welfare reforms were already in train before the war - reflected a deeper shift towards central planning, conformity, and an almost religious belief in bureaucratic solutions to society's miseries. The war, of course, had been the bureaucrat's dream; never in Britain's history had the country been so controlled by anonymous central powers dictating the lives of ordinary citizens. Conscription, rationing, evacuation of children, blackout precautions, requisitioning of property, watering of beer. And a huge hike in income tax. These measures, and many like them, were doubtless the source of much grumbling but they were generally accepted as necessary 'for the period of the emergency' and they became, after six years of war, so commonplace that by 1945 the people of Britain were well and truly softened up for a future determined by rules, regulations and civil servants. Perhaps no longer doffing their caps to the Lord of the Manor or the heartless factory owner they would instead kneel to Whitehall's regiments of economists, planners and social engineers. In short, to the people who knew what was best for you.

I'm not suggesting this was always a bad thing. Great things were achieved in the immediate post-war years and Britain was becoming for many people a fairer, healthier and more secure place to live, work and bring up a family.

But compared with the open spaces of Africa, which Dad had tasted and left behind, life 'back home' must have lacked flavour. Yes, he had a secure job and no doubt he might have worked his way up the ladder, but the horizons of opportunity still looked cramped and grey. His thoughts turned, for a second time, to emigration. Around this time Dad's eldest brother Harold, followed soon after by his sister Jean left England for Tasmania. Since 1945 Australia had actively encouraged Britons (and in smaller numbers, other Europeans) to emigrate to their land, promising a golden future with plentiful jobs, endless sunshine and the chance of owning your own home. As if that wasn't enough, the Australian government added the incentive of an assisted passage. They subsidised the fare for the long sea voyage so that an adult migrant had only to pay £10 (about £400 in 2018 money) while the kids travelled for free.

The Assisted Passage Migration Scheme supported one of the biggest planned migrations in history; it was a central tool in Australia's drive to 'Populate or Perish', and by populating it meant stocking up the country with the skilled workers it needed in a time of massive industrial growth. It also meant that the welcome was extended only to people of a desired 'type'. Thanks to the White Australia policy which operated in parallel, Black and Asian folk were not eligible to apply.

I think Dad was already looking into this within a few months of his return from Africa. What caught his eye was an opportunity to work on the Snowy Mountains Scheme in south-eastern Australia. True to the spirit of grand projects like the damming of the Tennessee valley in the 1930s and 1940s, the scheme would dam the Snowy River for agricultural irrigation and hydro-electric power. It became the biggest industrial project in Australia's history, building sixteen major dams and seven power plants over the following quarter-century. It was going to need a lot of manpower and the architects of the scheme came up with a neat solution to the problem of hiring the thousands of skilled workers and finding homes for them and their families on-site. The project was called Operation Snail.

The 'snail' name comes from the idea of a snail carrying its house on its back. Workers hired into the Snowy Mountain Scheme, like others a few years earlier who had been recruited to work on Australia's railways, would travel out to Australia by assisted passage with their pre-fabricated home carried out by ship – possibly the same ship – and assembled on arrival at one of the new communities which were germinating around the work sites. For Mum and Dad it must have looked pretty attractive at the time.

But they never went, and we are left with another unanswerable 'why?' 'We got cold feet' was all I was ever told. It wasn't the cold feet of a timid and unadventurous couple clinging to home. They had already been to Africa, after all, and in the end it was Africa that lured them back. A Plan B emerged: from Southern Rhodesia, today's Zimbabwe, Dad was offered a job with the municipal electricity department in the capital Salisbury (now called Harare). Perhaps, talking it through over endless cups of tea, Mum and Dad felt that life in an established colonial city was more tempting than a pre-fab in the wild mountains of Australia.

At this point we re-enter the world of family folklore – one of those Dad-stories whose veracity we always doubted yet always, even now, hoped to be true. In October 1951, after less than two years back in England, Dad was on his way back to Africa and he was to travel alone while the rest of the family would follow a few months later. He must have been up against a deadline because he decided he had to fly instead of taking the journey by ship and train which would use up almost three weeks of his time. A BOAC flight would get him to his destination from London Airport - as we used to call Heathrow before the expansion of Gatwick and Stansted –

in less than three days. The only snag was the fare. Nowadays you can fly that journey one-way for under £600; that equates to about a week's wages for the average working adult in Britain. Not so in 1951. The ticket would have set Dad back almost £200, the equivalent of over £6,000 in today's money. Thankfully the airline offered an option unheard of now, the standby fare. If you were prepared to take your chances, you could buy a standby ticket and hope that there would be a spare seat. If the flight was full, you could try again the next day. With standby tickets at a fraction of the full price, Dad had his chance to fly in an aeroplane for the first time in his life. He was almost thirty years old.

Luck was on his side and on the appointed day he was able to walk across the tarmac with the better-heeled full-fare passengers to board a BOAC Argonaut. It would be another year before BOAC entered the jet age and the Argonaut, the company's main workhorse at that time, was powered by four noisy Merlin engines originally developed for the Spitfire and the Lancaster. The aeroplane had fifty seats in one class and, according to Dad, it had a little cocktail bar at the back of the cabin. This much is true; you can Google it. The next part I can't verify. Dad always claimed that he sat next to Graham Greene and that the Oscar-winning film star Vivien Leigh was also travelling on the flight. If true, Dad could have engaged in small talk through the long hours in the air and asked Greene – shouting over the noise of the engines - what he was working on that year. 'We haven't decided on the title yet,' he might have replied, 'perhaps The End of the Affair'. Likewise Vivien Leigh - Mrs Laurence Olivier - may have accepted a light from my Dad, puffed on her cigarette and regaled him with recent gossip from the set of A Streetcar Named Desire.

Again, we will never know.

FIVE

Most people under the age of fifty will struggle to recall the pre-independence names of former British possessions. Ghana was Gold Coast. Lesotho was Basutoland. Tanzania was Tanganyika. Botswana was Bechuanaland. Between 1956 and 1968 every African colony and protectorate ruled by Britain was granted independent status, a result of deliberate British government policies formulated and adapted in the face of multiple pressures: nationalist movements, international opinion and, above all, a recognition of Britain's diminishing power. For the new states emerging from the process a change of name was an assertion of their fresh identity.

While many of these countries keep a low profile, everyone these days has heard of Zimbabwe, formerly Southern Rhodesia, and the name of its first black leader, the infamous Robert Mugabe. Zimbabwe's story is heart-breaking; from 1965 until 1980 it was involved in an increasingly brutal civil war while a white government led by Ian Smith, rebelling from British authority, attempted to resist the rule of the black majority. After 1980, in a deal brokered by the new government of Margaret Thatcher,

Mugabe came to power and after a brief honeymoon period the new country succumbed to tribal genocide, the embedding of a de facto single-party dictatorship and economic ruin. Mugabe maintained his grip on Zimbabwe until 2017 when he was finally ousted by his own party. Given that he was replaced by Emmerson Mnangagwa, known as 'the crocodile' and allegedly one of the brains (with Mugabe) behind the massacre of thousands of Ndebele people in the 1980's, poor Zimbabwe's future is uncertain.

Back in February 1952, when Mum, Tony and Stewart arrived in Southern Rhodesia's capital, the Union Jack was still flying and the horrors of future decades unimagined. Mr Mugabe (two years younger than Dad) was just another mission-educated schoolteacher recently returned from university in South Africa. White immigrants were being actively encouraged to settle in the country at that time because it had, outside South Africa, the most developed economy in the continent and it was believed to have great agricultural and industrial potential. In parallel thousands of black Africans were moving from their rural villages to work in the towns and cities. Salisbury was struggling to accommodate the growing population; this meant that for the first few months my family had to live in a hostel for new (white) immigrants. Tony was now six years old (and always, according to our parents, a precocious child) so his memories of that period were quite clear. This is what he later wrote about the place:

'Our first home was awful, we lived in a single storey L shaped block of 2 room flats and we shared the bathroom with another 8 or so families. This was a sort of hostel for new immigrants – everyone else were Afrikaners who had left South Africa. I'm sure that there are many good Afrikaners but these people sealed my feelings to this day, they were quite the most ignorant people you could ever have the misfortune to meet. '

Later in my own life I met and made sound friendships with 'many good Afrikaners' but I pass no judgement on

Tony's opinions. He recounted similar feelings towards 'the other white tribe' when he talked about his days as a teenage boarder at Milton High School in Bulawayo – the same school attended three decades earlier by Hendrik Verwoerd. Verwoerd went on to become (on the very day I was born, as it happens) the Prime Minister of South Africa and he is remembered now as the architect of Apartheid.

Stewart and Tony still managed to amuse themselves during their spell in the hostel. Mum remembered a morning when Tony came into their kitchen on the third floor of the building and asked, with convincing innocence, where Stewart was. Mum looked out at the tiny balcony and the deadly drop to the yard below. In a moment of pure maternal panic she ran down the stairs to the neighbour below and screamed 'Have you seen Stewart going past your window? ' Almost as soon as she had said it she realised the futility of the question, and shortly afterwards Stewart put her out of her misery by strolling in with a big grin. Tony had persuaded him to hide in the laundry basket and they all – except Mum – thought it was terribly funny.

After a few months the time in the Salisbury hostel came to an end and the family moved into a rented home. The large bungalow at 222 Jameson Avenue (now Samora Machel Avenue) was, as Tony put it, their 'first real house'. Mum and Dad had been married for nearly ten years and at last they had a place they could call their own. There was a new fridge, their first, and a living room carpet bought from the furniture shop owned by their neighbours, the Hammersteins. Tony started going to nearby David Livingstone Primary School while Stewart, still a pre-schooler, stayed at home with Mum. Dad went out to work each day, in the service of the city municipality, installing and repairing street lighting and other electrical services. I have a type-written letter which states that his conduct was 'extremely good' during those two years of service.

As far as I know Dad suffered only one personal mishap in the course of his duty. One day he opened the metal panel in the base of a street lamp to do some repairs to the wiring. The space behind the panel, he found, was filled by a hornet's nest. Hundreds of indignant occupants launched themselves at the intruder and pursued him as a pack along the street. By the time they gave up the chase he was literally covered in stings. Apart from the pain, the massive dose of hornet venom made him feel ill, so he went straight home. Mum took his clothes off him, parked him in a cool bath and spent the rest of the afternoon with a pair of tweezers extracting the stings from his flesh.

Hornets apart, life in Southern Rhodesia was pretty good for white people, even for working-class families like ours. Much has been written about white privilege in colonial Africa; it attempts to explain how it had been attained, how it was maintained, and the workings of the complex forces - already at work in the 1950s - which would eventually sweep it away. These accounts form a tangle of interlocking and sometimes contradictory narratives. Being neither a sociologist, a historian nor a political scientist I'm far from qualified to better them. Even if I tried, I would inevitably cast an ideological slant across the story (many already have, and still do) with a clumsy effort to shoe-horn events, attitudes, people and places into this or that theoretical position or to satisfy some unacknowledged prejudice. Would you gain a clearer picture of my family and the flesh-and-blood lives of their fellow whites and blacks, Jews and Gentiles and Hindus, the speakers of Afrikaans and Ndebele and English and Shona and Hindi? I don't think so, but it depends what you want.

Social media is awash with groups, blogs and other forums where people with an interest in Central Africa share their memories, opinions, images, loves, hates, facts and fictions. I'm grateful to all the people who participate, because they each cast a light – be it straight and true or distorted and shadowy – on a time and place central to my Dad's life. Through them I have made connections, filled in gaps, re-kindled memories and re-evaluated long-held assumptions. We have swapped stories: mostly trivial but all precious in their way. I have been reminded of the smell of the African soil after rain and how the love of that soil becomes embedded in the hearts of people who have inhabited that place.

And there have been moments of comedy; one day I mischievously replied to a Facebook post, which enquired how to renew an expired Zambian driving licence, by asking the same question and posting a picture of my Dad's own licence which had expired in 1968. A serious-minded but helpful respondent pointed out in some detail the changes in procedure and the bureaucratic obstacles to licence renewal after a fifty-year interval. When I thanked him and admitted that it had only been my feeble attempt at a joke, he quickly replied 'I thought so. '

But I also found that this corner of the social network, like so many others, has a darker aspect. While most participants keep their online activity balanced, friendly and genuinely informative a small but vocal segment use the medium to transmit (receiving is not in their nature) and re-cycle fossilised versions of the past. What ensues, with tedious predictability, is a game of willy-waving - we can fairly call it that as the antagonists are mostly male – between two opposing camps.

The first camp remembers Rhodesia the Glorious. She stood firm against interfering busybodies who 'didn't understand Africa'. She fought the communists when others wavered. She worked hard, farmed the land, toiled in the mines. She was firm but fair; sacrifices were made so the blacks could get some education (but not enough to disturb their equilibrium). She respected the tribal Chiefs and controlled the troublemakers. Everyone knew their place.

But she was sold down the river. There were enemies without and traitors within. She was robbed and raped by Mugabe and his cronies. How much more evidence did you need that Ian Smith – Good Old Smitty – had been right all along?

The second camp likes to talk about Heroes and Comrades. The Struggle. Black brothers, united, fighting side by side against the oppressors. The unredeemable wickedness of the white man. The blessings of victory, the restoration of dignity, the justifiable re-claiming of 'their' land. African Socialism.

Neither the Rhodesia the Glorious crowd (I'll call them RTG) nor the Heroes and Comrades (HAC) will concede an inch to the other side. Did white Rhodesians establish a dynamic economy and a sound infrastructure which benefited, more or less, all the inhabitants? HAC is deaf to the question. Was the dignity and aspiration of black people systematically extinguished by white minority rule? A small price to pay for stability and prosperity, says RTG. Was it hypocritical to conduct a war of liberation funded and trained by illiberal regimes, oppressors of their own people, like North Korea, China and the USSR? They were our socialist brothers, remembers HAC.

The questions go on, unanswered. Did the imprisonment and torture of political opponents really reflect the 'civilised standards' espoused again and again by Ian Smith? Can continuing loyalty to the 'liberators' be justified after decades of intimidation, hunger, genocide and theft?

You might argue that I am being unfair to the willy-wavers. I never had to live as a black second-class citizen under Smith or a white second-class citizen under Mugabe. My farm wasn't stolen, my daughter murdered by the invaders. My son wasn't shot in the back by the Selous Scouts. Emotion is inevitable. But, as I scroll through the posts and counter-posts, I wonder where all the shouting is supposed to lead. No-one seriously intends to change anyone's mind; if they did they would be asking questions, trying to learn and understand. Instead it's all sound and fury.

***

I am always attracted to 'alternative histories' – novels set in a time and place where past events have turned out differently. These stories come in a range of flavours; some focus on a twist in technology; Steampunk, for example, is a whole genre of its own which exploits the novelty of worlds where inventions like the internal combustion engine and the aeroplane have never appeared and the world is dependent upon – you guessed – steam. It's a sort of Edwardian time warp with skies full of airships, blokes in leather flying goggles and adventurous young women running around in tight corsets.

Other sub-genres pivot around alternative turns of events, like the Nazis winning the Second World War or Christian Europe never experiencing the Reformation. A lot of it is rubbish, but some of it is captivating, and it's no surprise that when I began to explore Dad's time in Central Africa I started to speculate about how the direction of change - and the final destination - could have turned out differently. What keeps coming back to my mind are the unanswerable questions about how different the past sixty years might have been if alternative decisions had been made or other policies adopted in the early days before African independence became a reality. Not a fictional steam-powered Africa – as an electrician Dad wouldn't have liked that – but a place where the transition from a colonial system could have been less divisive, less violent.

The more I looked, the more I found that there were many men and women, contemporaries of my Mum and Dad, who shared that vision. One of these was the man who became Prime Minister of Southern Rhodesia during the second year that my family lived there. His name was

Garfield Todd, a New Zealander who first went to Southern Rhodesia as a missionary in the 1930s and established, with his wife Grace, a thriving Christian community with a vast cattle farm, schools and clinics. He became a respected figure, admired by both blacks and whites. He believed passionately in the equality of all peoples; his daughter Judith remembered the colour-blindness of her upbringing on her father's Dadaya mission, a powerful influence which would shape her own life in Rhodesian politics.

Todd entered politics as an MP in 1946, believing that the cause of the black people of Rhodesia could be best served from within the white-controlled establishment. Despite being known as 'soft on the blacks', he maintained the support of many whites and by 1953 he was Prime Minister. Maintaining that support, however, was a delicate game. Within his cabinet and across the white community – remember that at that time it was only whites who had any meaningful representation – feelings were mixed about the question of black rights. Todd was supported by progressive-thinking cabinet allies like the former RAF pilot Hardwicke Holderness, but men like him were in the minority. There was intense debate on constitutional issues, not least in the complex matter of the franchise, where Todd attempted to nudge the system in favour of greater participation by blacks.

Ultimately, this proved a step too far for the white establishment and the people they represented. Todd was ousted in 1958 – the year Holderness has called the 'lost chance' – and the Southern Rhodesian government shifted steadily in the opposite direction. In 1965 it took the unprecedented step of unilaterally declaring its independence from Britain, digging in its heels against the tide of black nationalism and leading the country to isolation and war.

If Todd had been successful, and the Southern Rhodesian franchise had been adapted to allow more black people into the political process, both as voters and representatives, where would the country be now? One of the arguments put forward by the 'progressives' of the time was that by accelerating multi-racial political advancement, moderate black leaders would gain status and responsibility at the expense of black 'extremists' who wanted to take a more revolutionary path. With hindsight we might envisage an outcome with power in the hands of people better than Mugabe and a multi-racial society free from hatred and division. And prosperity in place of the economic catastrophes of 'socialism', land grabs and the greed of the elites.

Perhaps it is pointless to speculate. I've already drifted too far from the immediate story of Dad's life. I asked Bill and Eileen Young, close family friends who met Mum and Dad after moving to Southern Rhodesia in the mid-fifties, how much interest young white people had in the country's politics at that time. Not much, they said. They were too busy getting on with their lives, and any changes which might disrupt the status quo seemed to be far in the future. Life was about earning a living, bringing up a family, enjoying yourself. It was about the episodes which form today's memories: Tony recalled the Coronation Day Parade, the visit of the Queen Mother and Princess Margaret, the football match between Dundee United and the Rhodesian national team. He remembered going to the pictures (John Wayne in The Flying Rednecks) and having his tonsils out. Mum remembered it all as the happiest time of her life, a housewife in a proper house for the first time, staying at home and bringing up two small boys. For her it was only tainted by an unfulfilled yearning for a baby girl.

I have tried without much success to learn more about Mum's life in that period. By the time I was old enough to observe what was going on we all understood that Mum had suffered quite a bit of ill health, but the details are hazy. It wasn't until I was a teenager that I learned that

Mum had had two mastectomies. Supposedly the first had been necessary after she had 'lost a baby'. I have a vague sense that this happened in Southern Rhodesia a few years after Stewart was born and that it had led to complications. The child may have been the much-wanted girl. The mastectomy had been botched. As to why Mum, sometime later, had to have a second mastectomy nobody seems to know.

Perhaps this lack of clarity reflects Mum's place as the lone female in a family of males. In the 1950s men didn't want to think about 'women's troubles' any more than they would have wanted to witness the birth of a child. They certainly wouldn't talk about these matters to their sons. For many years, I can see now, Mum probably suffered in silence. But she loved her family, and even after the trauma of losing a child she didn't give up on hopes of having another.

For that, she would have to wait a few more years. But meanwhile Dad wasn't letting the grass grow under his feet. In Salisbury he was a Town Electrician, but in August 1953 he was offered a position as *the* Town Electrician. Not for Salisbury, but Que Que, a small mining town in the centre of the country, a hundred miles to the south-west. Once more, Mum had to pack up the crockery and the family prepared for another move. They had lived in Salisbury for just eighteen months.

SIX

For the next seven or eight years of Dad's life I can refer, gratefully, to the written account left behind by my brother. By the time the family arrived in their new home in Que Que Tony was in his eighth year and later, as an adult, he retained clear memories from that phase of his childhood. There are lots of vivid details and a definite sense of the Bulls moving up in the world.

The town of Que Que grew up from almost nothing when gold was discovered in the 1890s. When I say 'discovered' I mean by the first Europeans; the Shona people had been mining there for gold, copper and iron long before the arrival of the whites. There was a village called Sebakwe which developed alongside the mines and was eventually re-named Que Que after the name of nearby Fort Kwekwe. In the 1950s it was still a growing mining centre and it had a substantial European population. To get a feel for life in a place like that, I can recommend a novel called Whitewashed Jacarandas by Diana Polisensky. The book is based on the life of Diana's father, a Jewish doctor who moved to Que Que in the late 1940s and it illuminates the oddities of Que Que's white social scene. Socially and physically separated from the local black people, the whites were then sub-divided into their own compartments. Class was ever-present. Tony remembers the reflected status of being 'best friends' with John Slight, a boy whose father was a doctor:

'They had a car and were considered very rich and posh. It was an honour for me to go around with the Slights and Mum always made sure I was clean… '

Class aside, each of Que Que's white tribes had their place, with Afrikaans-speakers, many of them farmers, keeping some distance in that British-run territory. The small Jewish community included many professionals and business-people so they had a degree of status while being not-quite in the social centre. There were also Asians who played their part in the business life of the town, as well as smaller numbers of other Europeans: Greeks, Italians, Portuguese and so on. The British, of course, were top dogs.

Tony recorded a string of anecdotes whose spirit is reflected over and over whenever you speak to white people of that generation who grew up in Africa. What everyone remembers is the freedom of a youngster to run around and explore, get into scrapes and experience nature in the wild.

I enjoyed going out with John when his dad went to his surgery at the nearby mine at Redhill. We would be left to do our own thing in this vast open cast iron mine which I remember had a huge railway network. We would ride the little trolleys (as in Blazing Saddles) and do dares which involved crawling over a railway bridge and looking down to the river which seemed to be a mile below.

I would walk to school with my friends and if one of us had a chameleon (we all did at one time) we would catch grasshoppers with our school trilby hats, pull off their back legs and place them in front of the chameleon. They would struggle about on their remaining stumps only to be consumed with a flash as the chameleon's tongue would dart out about three inches and drag them in. A miserable way to go but we thought it was fun.

Eight-year-olds unsupervised in an open cast mine?

Carrying chameleons to school? It sounds almost as strange as your child wearing a trilby. For his part, Dad had another encounter with wildlife while he was out on the road working in Que Que. The family still couldn't afford a car, but one of the privileges of Dad's job was the use of a Ford pickup. One day during the rainy season Dad was out in the truck with his gang of African workmen. There had been some heavy rain and when he drove through an especially deep puddle the engine stopped. As this was in the days before WD40 he got out of the cab armed with a rag to dry off the electrics and when he opened the bonnet he was greeted by a King Cobra. The snake, disturbed in its warm spot by the engine, reared up to strike. Dad threw the rag at the snake and ran. When the Cobra emerged from under the back of the truck Dad's men jumped out and flattened it. African people have no time for snakes.

Considering that Africa is renowned for its dangerous reptiles, Dad's story includes very few. There will be one more snake tale, but that is in the future and three hundred miles to the north. Likewise with the six and eight-legged creatures that we normally associate with the tropics. We certainly saw a variety of creepy-crawlies, from huge moths to monster millipedes (tsongololos), super-fast hunting spiders and the infamous hornets, but very few gave the family any trouble. According to my brother they had scorpions living in the cracked plasterwork of their bedrooms in Que Que but I don't recall anyone saying they got stung. During my own childhood I only saw one living scorpion, a big black beast which Mum unearthed when she lifted a box of seedlings from outside our kitchen door in Lusaka. She screamed – unusual for Mum as she was pretty fearless – and by the time I had rushed onto the scene the scorpion was showing just how angry it was, with its tail raised and the sting pumped full of venom. Benson, our houseboy (that's the term people used for a male house-servant in those days) came to the rescue and started to bash it with a spade, but it wasn't going to give up without a fight. It hammered its sting against the spade, over and over, until Benson eventually managed to chop the creature in half. He then cut off the tail and popped it in his pocket, explaining that his uncle, a witch doctor of some sort, would be grateful for the sting. We didn't like to ask what he might be using it for.

That incident occurred in another place much later, after I was added to the brood. Meanwhile back in the family's Que Que years there was a temporary addition to the household. Mum's widowed mother, our Nana Stewart was invited to come to Africa and live with Mum and Dad. Apart from one or two photographs which give evidence that she was there, I know almost nothing about that shift in family life. Tony wrote about the overnight journey in a rented car to collect her from the railway station in Bulawayo and the excitement of meeting an elephant in the middle of the road (which turned out, up-close, to be a parked steam-roller). Mum told me how her mother, fresh out of England, couldn't get used to having a black servant in the house. She insisting on ironing her own 'smalls' when the houseboy normally did all the family's ironing. What she didn't realise is that after the laundry comes off the washing line, you have to iron everything really thoroughly in order to kill the eggs laid in the fabric by Putzi Flies. If you don't, as Nana Stewart found out by personal experience, the tiny fly larvae hatch in the seams of your clothes while you are wearing them, burrow silently into your skin and a few days later a boil develops which eventually erupts with pus and blood and a live maggot wriggling in its core.

Tony also remembered a rare row between Mum and Dad - followed by three days without the grown-ups speaking to each other – which he suspected had something to do with the intrusion of Nana Stewart into the family unit. A few months later she was on a ship back to England and normal life resumed. At that time, besides getting rid of his mother-in-law, I don't know if Dad had any sort of plan or vision for the future. I assume that he had moved to Que Que from Salisbury for the simple motive of a job with better pay. Otherwise it wouldn't have been worth the trouble of constantly moving house and, for my brothers, moving schools. Or perhaps I misjudge Dad's motives and in fact he was simply a man with itchy feet – not unlike me – always on the lookout for something new.

In the 1950s Southern Rhodesia was changing fast, a place of opportunity. Having established itself as one of Britain's most developed African possessions, its potential underpinned by the richness of its mineral resources and the fertility of the agricultural land, it had been granted self-governing status in 1923. What 'self-governing' meant in practice was to have major implications over the following decades. Since the nineteenth century, in those places within the British Empire which had significant settler populations, there had been movement towards a principle known as Responsible Government. This led to the establishment of administrations and forms of representation increasingly autonomous from the central power of Westminster, and it ultimately gave birth to the great Dominions of Canada, Australia, New Zealand and South Africa.

In the early part of the twentieth century Southern Rhodesia's political parties were divided into two camps: those in favour, and those against, the incorporation of the colony into the Union of South Africa. In a referendum in 1922 the 'against' argument prevailed and Southern Rhodesia was permitted to remain a separate entity with a new, semi-independent elected assembly, albeit with important powers retained by the Crown. Election to the assembly (and qualification as a candidate) was based upon a theoretically non-racial, gender-free franchise; to qualify, the voter or candidate simply had to have been resident in Southern Rhodesia for at least six months, demonstrate a command of written English, and either occupy property worth £150 in their electoral district or receive an annual salary of £100 within the colony. Interestingly there was another qualification for non-residents – they too could qualify if they owned a registered mining claim within the colony, which said a lot about where the power lay.

If you wonder why I'm drifting back into politics, bear with me. However much, or little, Dad might have paid attention to electoral systems or policies or changes of government while he was working to keep the lights on in Que Que, these things would soon affect the course of his life and continue to do so until he eventually left Africa for the last time twenty years later. Consider the question of the franchise. Since 1918 British subjects at home had had 'one man, one vote' – including, for the first time, votes for women - with no qualifications for men except to be over the age of twenty-one. By 1928 all remaining qualifications were lifted for women and they finally achieved electoral equality with men. But the set-up in Southern Rhodesia looked more like Victorian Britain where only a small minority had been qualified to vote and – as well as all the women - most working class men were excluded. What this meant in Southern Rhodesia was that if you wanted to vote, or put yourself up for election, you had to be white. Only a tiny minority of the black population could meet the criteria for property occupancy or income.

The result – it's obvious – was a white-run government for a piece of the world (supposedly 'self-governing') where 95% of the people were black. And that meant that the future direction of the colony would be determined by the white politicians and the aspirations of the white adults who elected them. This is not to say that every policy, every law, was automatically driven by white self-interest. But within that system, in 1953, a critical decision was taken which would lead Southern Rhodesia in a new direction and shape the lives of its people and its central

African neighbours for years to come.

Once it had been decided that the colony would not be swallowed up by South Africa, an argument took root which asserted that Southern Rhodesia's future prosperity depended on closer economic ties with neighbouring British possessions to the north, Northern Rhodesia and Nyasaland. Less developed, less industrialised and with smaller numbers of white settlers, those colonial territories still had significant natural resources which included some of the world's richest copper mines. In 1953 the arguments came to fruition when the British government approved the formation of the Federation of Rhodesia and Nyasaland. The idea was to harness the industrial capacity of Southern Rhodesia to the resources of the north, although Nyasaland – a much smaller partner – had little to offer in comparison with the Northern Rhodesian Copperbelt. And there were no illusions about the Federation being a partnership of equals, whatever its new constitution might say. Southern Rhodesia was in the driving seat, and the Federal Capital would be in Salisbury.

For Dad, the formation of the Federation was an opportunity. While each of the three partner countries (technically, a self-governing colony and two protectorates) was to retain its own form of local colonial government, the armed forces would come under direct Federal command. The need to develop a Federal army to bolster the existing mix of regiments supplemented by British Army units led to a recruitment drive and Dad, who had genuinely enjoyed his wartime service with the Royal Marines, was keen to get back into uniform. He wouldn't have to start at the bottom – as a former marine, a qualified armourer, and white, he could join as a Sergeant. And there would be other perks like a married quarter for his family, free medical care and so on.

So at the end of 1954 it was goodbye to Que Que and back to Salisbury. For Mum, another house move to organise, one of many more to come. She wasn't to know at the time, but there would be at least a dozen more moves before she settled into her brief old age, and an unimaginable number of tea chests to be filled and emptied. Yet she managed to take it all in her stride with a dependable knack of turning each new place, big or small, into a family home. Throughout all our upheavals I think that gave a measure of security to my brothers and me. We quickly recognised Mum's pictures and ornaments in each unfamiliar place and old curtains adapted to hang in new windows.

Returning to Salisbury Dad again preceded the rest of the family by a few months, probably so the boys could finish the school year which runs from January to December in that part of the world. For all the efforts which my parents would have made to help Tony and Stewart adapt, it was not a smooth move for Tony. While he remembered such happy times in Que Que, this is what he wrote about the first year in Salisbury:

I went to Alfred Beit School where, for reasons I still don't understand, I was bullied relentlessly. I hated it - perhaps being English and a bit of a weed had something to do with it. We had a lodger whose name I don't know, and for Christmas 1955 I was given Meccano #4 which Dad and the lodger broke. '

Such are the ups and downs of life when you are nine years old. Stewart, at six, may have found things a little easier because he had (and still has) a more easy-going disposition. As for Mum and Dad, the change of direction suited them. Dad was appointed to the Staff Corps of the new Federal Army and Mum, in keeping with the times, became very much the Army Wife. She welcomed the chance to make new friends, the wifely camaraderie of the Sergeants' Mess, the dances and parties and tombola nights. And Christmas parties for the children; even Dad took his turn to play Santa, an unlikely choice as he never weighed more than ten stone, but sufficiently disguised to fool his own son. When he sat on the knee of the man in the red suit, unaware of Santa's true identity, Tony lied through his teeth when he was asked if he had been a good boy and behaved kindly to his little brother.

I have a number of photographs from that time. Lots of Dad in his uniform: sparkling brown shoes, long socks with the regimental flash, classic khaki shirt and shorts with creases ironed like razors. Aussie-style bush hat with the brim turn up on one side. Out of those pictures shines his pride in bearing the uniform, especially in his passport photograph where, with his dark moustache and near-Mediterranean complexion, he looks rather like that nemesis of the British Empire, Egypt's Colonel Nasser.

Eight years after demobilisation from the Royal Marines Dad was once again back in the armourer's workshop. Time-worn Lee Enfield .303s and the new Belgian-designed SLRs. Bren guns, GPMGs, Sten and Sterling sub-machine guns and Browning automatic pistols. Three-inch mortars and hand grenades. Keeping all this hardware in working order would become Dad's bread and butter for another nineteen years; as a result my brothers and I would grow up soaked in the language of arms and ammunition. We regularly visited Dad at work and he allowed us to hang around the armouries and workshops, smelling the linseed oil as it was rubbed into the wooden stocks of the rifles and the acrid stench from the bluing tanks, where rubber-gloved armourers immersed the steel parts of the weapons in powerful chemicals. Dad took us to open-air and indoor firing ranges and sometimes, better than any treat imaginable for a youngster, allowed us to fire some of the weapons. My favourite, at the age of nine or ten, was a Heckler and Koch HK42 submachine gun. The weight and power of the thing in my hands, the smell of cordite and the clatter of empty cartridges lives with me now. My hearing has probably never recovered.

All the main army bases had armouries, so inevitably the armourers found themselves posted around the Federation. After a year based in Salisbury Dad was sent to

Lusaka, the capital of Northern Rhodesia. To white Southern Rhodesians, most of whom had never been there, it was the Black North, a label for a territory where the whites were even more outnumbered than in the south. It also had connotations of a primitive, backward place which according to some standards it probably was, relatively, although I don't believe Dad or Mum had any qualms about moving there. It was just another adventure.

Tony remembered the journey from south to north in the family's first car, a black 1949 Morris Minor and a small signifier of the Bull's growing affluence. The roads may have been better-kept than they are now but they were still pretty primitive and it would have been a hot and uncomfortable ride for a family of four. Crossing the Zambezi River at Chirundu the car was sprayed with DDT – with the occupants baking inside with all the windows shut – as a measure to control the spread of the Tsetse fly. The Morris Minor was now in Northern Rhodesia, on the last leg towards what Tony called 'Lusaka, our new and very happy home.' For him Lusaka meant an escape from the bullies in Salisbury, and for me, two years later, a place to be born.

Back in uniform.

The photo of the spear-bearers was taken at Fort Rosebery (now called Mansa) in Northern Rhodesia.

Dad is second from right.

A father with two
sons.

And then three.
The author is the
one not smiling.

SEVEN

Family life in Lusaka meant life on 'the camp'. Arakan Barracks was named after the Third Arakan Campaign of the Second World War, when the men of the Northern Rhodesia Regiment – the NRR - had fought so valiantly against the Japanese in western Burma. The married quarters were located within the perimeter of the camp and Mum and Dad were allocated an Altum, a basic type of corrugated iron house. Later, they moved into a bigger home with a separate kitchen out-house furnished with a wood-fuel stove. I remember Mum, who was never the most confident cook, saying what a challenge it was getting that truculent stove fired up to prepare the family meals.

In those pre-independence days the army was a mix of local and British Army men and units. All, of course, pledged allegiance to the Crown but the regiments like the NRR which were now directly serving the Federation had a more local character, drawing almost all of the troops from the local black population while many of the NCOs were white men with roots in Central Africa. Nonetheless, the majority of the officers were seconded from the British Army. From time to time the barracks in Lusaka also hosted battalions from the King's African Rifles which included black soldiers from other parts of Africa; during the 1950s these units were regularly deployed to Malaya as part of Britain's long running campaign against communist insurgents. According to Mum, the wives of NCOs who had spent time in Malaya were 'a bit superior', bragging about their servants and showing off their fancy far-eastern furniture. They had taken a backward step by coming to Lusaka and they wanted you to know it.

Stewart and Tony settled into a new school, Woodlands, where I would start my own primary education eight years later. It may have been 6,000 miles from London but the flavour of the place was marked by English routines like inter-house cricket; every week the Angles (Tony became their House Captain) played the Saxons. The Woodlands suburb which surrounded the school had its roads named to reinforce the bond with the mother country: Westminster, Ripon, York, Birch, Cedar and the like. The city was determined to be more Home Counties than Black North. The army, in similar fashion, upheld the symbols and practices of home – beating the retreat, raising the colours, a fife-and-drum band. The annual Queen's Birthday Parade, one of Mum's favourite occasions. Lusaka in the late fifties truly was the 'happy place' for my family. Dad loved his work and Mum was in her element bringing up two small boys in that benign and comfortable environment. Only in October – the Suicide Month - did the climate become oppressively hot, and it was swiftly relieved by the rains in November. Out of the red earth grew Jacaranda, Frangipani, Paw Paw, Hibiscus, Bougainvillea. Everywhere there was light and colour, broad open spaces, an enormous sky. It was, and still is, a beautiful sunlit place.

I have read dozens of accounts of the lives of white families who lived in Northern Rhodesia. When I compare them with our own memories I am struck by the realisation that my parents, in spite of taking themselves off to the heart of Africa, were not particularly adventurous people. While many took every opportunity to travel the country, camp out, take safaris and – frequently – shoot the wildlife, my Mum and Dad were mostly content to while away their spare time at home, playing with the children, listening to the radiogram, drinking tea and entertaining friends. There were no encounters with crocodiles or treks through the bush. Maybe this is a false comparison; those who did the adventuring were perhaps more likely to record their expeditions in diaries and letters and there have been many more who, like Mum and Dad, simply wanted the quite life. I asked Dad's close friend Bill Young about this – he and his wife Eileen seemed to have enjoyed some excitement in their travels – and he suggested to me that wherever you lived, your time was mostly taken up with work and the day-to-day responsibilities of life. It made no difference that you were in the heart of Africa.

Perhaps Dad's younger life also had something to do with it. Having grown up in a not-quite-poor family he simply wanted to make the most of the relative comfort and affluence he was starting to enjoy in his thirties. Maybe that was the limit of his horizon; he didn't need to prove anything by trekking up-country and killing an elephant. He would rather light a cigarette, close his eyes and listen to Frank Sinatra or Nat King Cole. He had seen enough killing in his twenties, facing the Germans and the Italians.

Not that the family always stayed in town. Stewart remembers fishing trips to the nearby Kafue River where, being a patient lad, he often caught a lot more fish than his older brother or any of the adults. Those trips were great social occasions with a convoy of family cars supplemented by a commandeered three-ton truck to carry all the kids and fishing gear and picnic rations. The river was shared with hippos and the occasional crocodile. It was on one of those outings that Dad received his first – I think his only – speeding ticket. On the way home after a long day by the river most of his buddies decided to stop off for a beer in the small town of Kafue, but Dad, the only non-drinker, pressed on towards home and tore through the town well over the speed limit. The Northern Rhodesia Police were waiting for him with their stopwatches and their eyeballs, the only technology they needed to gather the evidence.

Now that Dad was in government service he was entitled to home leave, and at the end of 1957 the family went back to England for a two month holiday. In those days if you travelled by sea you had to go a long way south from landlocked Lusaka before you could sail north to Europe. The journey on the steam-hauled sleeper took at least two days by Rhodesia Railways, routing through Livingstone and on to Bulawayo where the passengers changed to *Suid-Afrikaanse Spoorwee* (South African Railways). There followed a further three days travelling via Bechuanaland, entering South Africa at Mafeking and onward to Cape Town where they would join the ship to Southampton. At regular stops the locomotive took on coal and water where, in some of the remote and dusty halts of Bechuanaland, the carriages were surrounded by local people selling trinkets and carvings, the passengers tossing their pennies from the windows.

The family enjoyed the holiday. As expected they stayed with Dad's parents at 82 Standard Road and Tony even joined the local Scout troop where his cousin Keith was a patrol leader. Mum and Dad must have been getting along well; I have calculated that I was conceived during the early part of that holiday which meant that poor Mum suffered from morning sickness throughout the sea voyage home. At the time it was explained away as seasickness and Tony and Stewart were not told the news about the baby until they arrived back in Lusaka. Before the holiday, Mum and Dad had told them that they were considering adopting a child from Hungary or the Congo, both places which had experienced bloodshed in 1956 and 1957 which had resulted in many children, it was believed, being orphaned. The 'adopted little sister plan' had to be abandoned when the biological baby was on its way. A disappointment for Mum, I was a boy.

At least this was Tony's account of my arrival in the world. Mum and Dad used to explain it differently, saying that they had already decided against adoption when it transpired that some of the babies being offered were not in fact orphans but whose parents had been temporarily displaced by the conflict in their home countries. Either way, I sometimes think how things could have turned out. If the adoption business had been processed a little quicker they might not have bothered having me and Mum may have got the daughter she longed for. Not that she stinted on maternal love when I arrived in September of 1958. I put her through a notably difficult labour and she was, by the standards of the day, an 'older mother' of thirty five. I was a weak baby, a scrap of just over five pounds who the nurses warned her may not survive. 'I was determined to prove them wrong', she told me. Well, here I am. Thank you Mum.

Because the married quarter provided by the army only had two bedrooms there had to be some re-arranging to accommodate a new baby. Lucky for the Bulls, they had a close family friend in Jimmy Harris, a public works contractor who divided up one of the rooms to create a nursery with a DIY frame for my carrycot and, soon after, a hand-made solid timber cot. The cot might not have met current safety standards; one night when I was four months old Mum found me half-strangled, hanging by my neck from the bars of the cot, inexplicably on the outside. I survived asphyxiation and added to the store of family anecdotes, this one often being told alongside another about my narrow escape from being crushed by a falling bookcase.

Hazards presented themselves outdoors too. We once had a photograph, now lost, of Mum next to a dead snake in 1959. This was the family-famous Puff Adder which she felt slithering over her foot one day while she was out in the garden. She had already heard a hissing noise and ignored it as it sounded like a lawn sprinkler. When she saw the creature on her foot she screamed and Stewart and Tony, who had been playing nearby outside the Sergeant's mess, ran to the scene.

'There's a snake in the bushes. Get Dad!'

The boys scampered back to the mess, where Dad, as Mess Treasurer, was working on the accounts. According to Tony Dad didn't at first believe them. It may have had something to do with Tony's already well-established reputation for tall tales and practical jokes. But eventually he responded and came home to find a fat Puff Adder, over a metre long, hiding under the Christ-thorn hedge. The word spread around the camp and soon the garden was full of people armed with personal handguns, mostly trophies from the Second World War. They blasted away at the hedge where the snake had taken refuge, the creature decided to come out and make a dash for it, and it was finally despatched with an ex-Nazi Luger. Somebody then cut it open – it was heavily pregnant – and skinned it. Mum had had a fortunate escape; the venomous *bitis arietans* kills more people in Africa than any other snake.

By now my brothers were getting quite grown up, with Tony starting senior school. Later in 1959 Dad was posted to Llewellyn Barracks in Bulawayo, the second city of Southern Rhodesia. Tony stayed on as a boarder at Gilbert Rennie School in Lusaka but was so miserable there – he had been placed in a school hostel 'filled with Afrikaner boys and housemasters' – that after a month he took the initiative to write home and put himself on a train to Bulawayo. He remembered a homecoming tempered by his parent's disappointment that they had spent so much money on a now-unusable school uniform.

Llewellyn Barracks was home to the Royal Rhodesia Regiment and a major army training depot. In future years it would see the training of hundreds of young soldiers, national servicemen and volunteers. By the mid-sixties and into the seventies the barracks would be producing the men who fought the bush war for Ian Smith's Rhodesia against the communist-backed armies of ZIPRA and ZANLA. In their day, after Rhodesia's unilateral declaration of independence, the Rhodesia Regiment had dropped the 'Royal' prefix but in Dad's time they still served the Queen. Bulawayo had a long legacy of British military training, with RAF Kumalo only recently closed after hosting thousands of trainee pilots during and after World War II as part of the British Commonwealth Air Training Plan. It was on the disused Kumalo runway that Dad taught Tony to drive in the second family car, a 1949 Austin. Mum, too, tried to learn there, but she quickly gave up. Her two older sons realised it would be fun to lift the back end of the car off the ground while Dad was trying to show her how to release the clutch and move off. Much spinning of the back wheels, great hilarity for Tony and Stewart. After that Mum never attempted driving again.

It had been a cruel outcome, given that Mum already lacked self-confidence in most areas of her life. Or, just as likely, she used the boys' prank as an excuse to stop trying. When she was older she often lamented her failure to tackle the skills which were being mastered by her female contemporaries; driving, typing, book-keeping, the range of activities which could propel a woman in those days – even with Mum's limited education - into the workplace. As kids we were too self-absorbed to notice. Mum was just Mum while Dad was somehow the one to be admired, the breadwinner with his work and his uniform and his robust good humour. Meanwhile Mum made sure we were fed and bathed and clothed, she nursed us when we were sick and she comforted us when we were hurt. Rarely did we give her any thanks for it, but Dad's appreciation for her was absolute.

Most people would remember Dad as a warm, open and generous man. At times his generosity got the better of him. Stewart recalled the invitation – supported by Mum – which Dad offered to a family they had met during their last sea voyage from England. The family was likewise on its way to Central Africa so Dad encouraged them to visit 'if ever you are in our area '. One day, at least a year after that brief acquaintance, the family turned up at our house in Bulawayo and asked if they could stay. Mum and Dad didn't hesitate with their hospitality, unaware that the family, once established, had little urgency to move on. They stayed for three months and took full advantage of Mum and Dad's kindness. Stewart's most painful memory was the children of the soon-to-be-unwanted guests wrecking all his toys. He doesn't remember how they were finally ejected.

I don't remember that episode. I must have been there, but it probably happened in 1959 or 1960 when I wasn't much more than a baby. By 1961 and 1962, when I was three or four, my earliest memories emerge and they all come from Bulawayo. I remember Tony being mostly absent; although his school, Milton was nearby he stayed there as a boarder. Stewart was still at home, in his final years at Fairbridge Primary School and my first true hero. Stewart was nine years older and he could do things I could barely imagine doing. He could whistle, and worked hard to show me how to do it. He could make things like catapults from bits of tree-branch and strips of inner tube. He could whittle wood with his own pen-knife. Above all, he went to the quarry. The quarry was a mythical location where boys of Stewart's age went after school. I was not permitted to go and I did not know what happened there. The mystery and excitement of this unseen place became an obsession for me; I begged and begged to go with Stewart but I wasn't allowed. I was too small.

One day I decided that there was only one way to satisfy this unfulfilled desire. Seeing Stewart leave the house and set off down the road, knowing he must be going there, I followed him. Not followed exactly – he was soon way ahead of me and I lost sight of him. But I plodded along in the heat in what I must have thought was the right direction. I was going to the quarry! And Mum hadn't seen me go. But before I had got very far a car pulled up beside me, driven by a white man. I don't remember who the man was but in that small community I guess he knew me. He asked me where I was going and I told him I was going to the quarry. He told me to get in his car and he took me home to my Mum. I never did see that quarry but even now, over fifty years later, I still try to locate it on Google Maps.

The school which Stewart attended had an ambiguous legacy. For many years it was considered one of the best schools in the area, a reputation which carried through beyond 1980 when it ceased to be a white-only institution. It was also, until 1965, a component of the Fairbridge Society, originally The Society for the Furtherance of Child Emigration to the Colonies. The society's founder was Kingsley Fairbridge, a South African born Englishman who moved to Southern Rhodesia in 1896. As a young man visiting Britain he was struck by the contrast between the overcrowding and deprivation of British cities with the open spaces of colonial Africa, sparking the idea of sending underprivileged children overseas where they would be trained to work in agriculture (if they were boys) or for the girls, domestic service. White stock would fill the underpopulated colonies, which were hungry for labour.

Fairbridge's vision led to the emigration of thousands of children to Southern Rhodesia, Canada, Australia, New Zealand and South Africa. Dozens of schools were established and no doubt for many the opportunity was positive and life-changing. But in recent years a troubled side to the story has emerged; many of the children and their parents were not consulted about joining the migration programme and in effect the children were forcibly moved. Many suffered abuse, neglect and exploitation at the hands of the institutions and families who received them, especially in Australia. None of this misery was apparent when Stewart attended the Bulawayo school set up to support the programme. It was only during Stewart's last two terms at the school, when he was a temporary boarder while Dad was re-posted to Salisbury, that he came to know two remaining 'Fairbridge Boys' who still resided in the school's dormitories. The Rhodesian part of the emigration programme was wound up a few years later.

As for Tony, he wrote a great deal about his Bulawayo years. In a land rich in stalactites and ores and crystals he became an amateur collector of minerals. At boarding school he experienced the perennial clash of cultures between English and Afrikaans, the beatings from his science teacher and the founding of strong friendships. He played rugby (for the 'D' teams) and listened to The Shadows and Del Shannon on the radio. He considered becoming a doctor. He came home for the holidays and in the Christmas break of 1961 we five piled into Dad's Opel Rekord station wagon for a trip to the seaside.

I now live a twenty-minute walk from the sea. From Bulawayo the closest piece of ocean is 500 miles away at Beira, a sea-port on the Indian Ocean which in 1961 was located in the Portuguese colony of Moçambique and a two-day drive from home. But we didn't go to exotic Beira; instead Dad opted to take us to the English-speaking seaside in South Africa, a thousand miles by road to Amanzimtoti near the city of Durban. For comfort en-route Dad had modified a spare mattress to fit into the boot of the car, which is where I roamed or slept in the carefree days before seatbelts. At the beach campsite I slept in there too, with Mum, while Dad and my brothers used an army tent. In Tony's account of the holiday he wrote that 'it rained all the time ' but I have a photo which shows us looking happy enough, sitting on the white sand and squinting in bright sunshine. Nevertheless during the first week Dad cut his foot badly on a piece of glass on the beach and the trip was terminated early. We drove home, arriving on Christmas Eve at a house with no decorations and no dinner.

I have another photograph from that trip of the five of us in a café somewhere along the road back to Southern Rhodesia. In the picture there is a wagon wheel hanging on the wall to signify the name of the café. It was the place where, as Mum periodically reminded me, my three-year-old self caused her acute embarrassment by asking, in a voice heard by all the other customers, if we would be putting up the tent again that night. The first time she told me that, I didn't understand the significance. It was only much later that I realised that in Mum's status-conscious eyes a family that camped, that slept in a tent, was a family that looked like it couldn't afford a hotel. For that to be revealed in public by your careless-mouthed toddler was no less than social suicide. Dad, on the other hand, couldn't have cared less.

EIGHT

Perhaps it is inevitable at this stage of the story that I am writing more about myself than about my Dad. I've been waiting in the wings, unborn, and I have memories of my own to share, not hand-me-downs. Not that that will make the story any more authentic; we all know how unreliable memory can be, particularly when it is shaped by years of re-telling in a decades-long game of Chinese Whispers.

Take the example of my first emergency visit to the doctor's surgery. I was around four years old and getting dressed, unsupervised, in my bedroom. Mum was in another room, talking to a friend. I inadvertently put both feet into the same leg of my shorts, forcing me to hop and jump like a rabbit or a kangaroo because my legs were squeezed together in one leg-hole and I couldn't walk properly. I thought this was fun and began to hop around the room, bumping into the furniture and shouting that I was Tickey the Clown. Before long I tripped and banged my head on the corner of an iron bedstead. Mum heard my cries and came into the room to find me with blood pouring from a gash in my temple.

I had two stitches in my head and I still have a small scar. How much of that episode is directly remembered, and how much is a groove in my brain created by Mum re-telling the story? Did I tell her at the time that I thought I was Tickey the Clown? Do I really remember the doctor stitching me up? I'm pretty sure I remember how much it hurt, and the blood pooling on the polished cement floor. But so much of the past is like this, fragmentary, and we have to make the best of it. These bits of recollection, some solid, others less so, are all we've got.

In the meantime you might be wondering who Tickey the Clown was. He was southern Africa's most famous circus performer and a children's icon throughout the Rhodesias, South Africa and Moçambique. I remember the thrill of seeing Boswell's Circus – and Tickey – when they visited Lusaka, probably sometime after my ill-judged impersonation. And a Tickey, while we are digressing, was also the name for a sixpence, a little silver coin we used in that part of the world before decimalisation.

I don't think that Dad would mind this part of his life story being co-opted by his kids and their encounters with clowns. His family resided at the centre of his world and whatever we got up to was every bit as important to him as anything that might be happening in grown-up land. I don't ever remember him being too tired or distracted to admire a drawing or a newly-completed Airfix model or to help me with my homework. He – and Mum - sweated to help me understand maths, which at one time used to reduce me to tears.

I recently read a newspaper cutting from a local paper which marked the celebration of Dad's parents' golden wedding anniversary in 1963. When the reporter asked the couple whether they belonged to any local clubs or societies they replied that 'our family is our club'. It was much the same for Dad; although he was active in army social life it didn't take him away from his wife and children any more than it needed to. He never went in for golf or any other lads-only diversions. Nor did he drink, which must have marked him out from most of his buddies although it never diminished his popularity. In truth, he wasn't 100% teetotal, but like me he was intolerant of alcohol and if he drank more than a very small amount it made him ill. I don't know if it was due to lack of practice – I have had friends who treat it like a sport, something they have to train for – or Dad's individual metabolism. According to Stewart it was put to the test when Dad left Llewellyn Barracks and was posted back to Salisbury. In Dad's honour there was a leaving 'do' in the Sergeant's Mess and to be polite Dad accepted, however reluctantly, some of the beers bought for him. But the drinks were spiked. Dad was so ill that he was completely incapacitated for three days after the party.

The return to Salisbury in 1962 was to be Dad's final posting in the Federal Army. The Federation of Rhodesia and Nyasaland had been formed in 1953 as a too-late colonial project to harness the resources of three adjacent territories and it soon became an anachronism during that fast-changing decade. Even at its inception there was vigorous opposition from a generation of young Black Nationalist leaders who saw the Federation as nothing more than a tool for buttressing white power. Their misgivings were voiced in Britain by politicians of the left like Tony Benn and John Stonehouse as well as a growing number of conservatives who recognised the hard facts of the day: Britain was declining as a world power and sound reasons for shedding the colonies were accumulating.

The mother country could no longer afford the administrative and military structure to uphold British rule overseas. Observing this, and ever the opportunists, the Soviet Union, the Peoples Republic of China and their own subject nations were united in declaring their opposition to all forms of 'imperialism', most publically in the United Nations where their voices were multiplied when newly independent states – notably India – joined the international community. The Soviet leaders did not blush at the irony in their pronouncements about 'liberation' while they enslaved their own people and their neighbours in Eastern Europe. Furthermore, Britain's supposed ally, the United States, was deliberately waging its own anti-colonial drive in an effort to break down the old economic order and penetrate markets hitherto protected for the benefit of Britain. In short, the game was up and Britain had to set about dismantling the empire.

Against this background it is a wonder that the Federation ever got off the ground in the first place. That it did shows up two important features of British rule in that part of Africa. First, the well-rooted conviction held by tens of thousands of white people - especially in Southern Rhodesia, where they had greater numbers - that the country had been built by them and their forbears and that they had worked hard to create a modern, civilised and peaceful society. It was 'theirs', and they intended to stay and retain power. Second, there was a growing social and intellectual divide between the white settler societies and their brothers and sisters 'back home'. The 1950s saw unprecedented social change in Britain, with shifting morals, diminishing respect for authority, rampant consumerism and growing numbers of immigrants. This contrasted with the world of the stereotypical white Rhodesian: he was hard-working and well-mannered, loyal to the Crown and deeply conservative, especially in matters of race. Even by the 1960s, when I was growing up in newly-independent Zambia, my parents frequently expressed their dismay at the behaviour of the people at home, the bra-burners and queer MPs and pot-smoking pop stars. Their disquiet was magnified, no doubt, by the fact that our main source of information was the News of the World, airmailed out every week by Dad's mother.

What this all meant was that while Westminster and Whitehall were busy engineering the orderly undoing of the empire, counterparts in central Africa were preparing, with equal determination, for decades of white-run development and prosperity and the managed suppression of black political aspiration. The idea of simply throwing it all away, handing the reins to upstart black activists, was unthinkable. They were seen as nothing more than opportunists, troublemakers who had only their personal interests at heart and who would hand the place over to the communists.

One of those feared black upstarts was Kenneth Kaunda, who would later become the first president of independent Zambia. In his book 'Black Government?', written while he was still agitating for an end to colonial rule in Northern Rhodesia, he described the contrast between his treatment as a black man in his own country and his experience of visiting Britain:

When travelling overseas in Britain, I was treated with courtesy everywhere. I was received in homes of the highest and the lowest, and suffered no social embarrassment. Back at home I remember going into a café in Kitwe. It was in April 1957. I went to the counter and asked for sandwiches, but was told "boys are not served here". I tried to reason with the assistant, that all I wanted was service, but without success. The next thing I knew I was being thrown outside by fellow customers... '

The indignity suffered by Kaunda was minor but typical of the many injustices of life in a segregated and unequal society. We shouldn't forget that this sort of thing sometimes happened in Britain too, but in the colonies it was embedded in the social and political structure and by the fifties and sixties it was becoming, in the eyes of much of the British establishment (including the notably vocal churches) unacceptable. Within the territories themselves these opinions were echoed by a small white minority, including the likes of former PM Garfield Todd and Guy Clutton-Brock in Southern Rhodesia and by John Moffat, Stewart Gore-Brown and the Reverend Colin Morris in Northern Rhodesia. But the majority of Europeans viewed these fellow-whites with suspicion or hostility. For many they were 'kaffir lovers', naïve idealists who didn't understand the risks involved in giving power to the blacks. My Dad might not have labelled them so crudely, but he would have shared the fears of their critics.

With hindsight we know that some of those fears were well-founded, given the dismal quality of many post-independence leaders, yet I can't avoid returning to the idea that if Todd and Moffat and their ilk had been given a hearing, history may have turned out more peaceably. Dad, I believe, would not have agreed with me; we were never one of the 'liberal white' families. On the other hand Dad was constant in showing respect to black Africans and avoiding the crude and pejorative language of some of his more racist contemporaries. From time to time we may have heard the words 'munt' and 'kaffir' in our house, but not from our parents' lips.

So the Federation was built, quarreled over, and by the time Dad was posted back to Salisbury in 1962, already in its dying days. The Federal Prime Minister, the rough-edged bruiser Sir Roy Welensky, bewailed the treachery of the British government. In the end even the Tories had let him down and left the way open for black majority rule. With all this talk of change Dad, now a Staff Sergeant, was starting to wonder where his army career would take him. His family were growing up. Tony was in his last year of school and had switched his career plan from medicine to the Royal Navy, odd for a boy who had grown up hundreds of miles from the sea. As Stewart remembers it, the relationship between Tony and Dad became difficult. Tony was home only during the holidays from boarding school and was beginning to see himself as an independent being, almost a man, who no longer need the guidance and instruction of parents. 'He always had to have the last word' summed up Dad's memories of his eldest son.

In truth, that was how we all remember Tony – he never grew out of the habit. But as a small child I only remember the love – bordering on hero-worship – which I felt for my bigger brothers. In Salisbury we lived in Tait Avenue and I will indulge in two personal anecdotes, nothing to do with Dad, from that family home. First, it was the place where I acquired my imaginary friend, a cowboy called Hosepipe. Therapists can make what they will of that. Mum and Dad humoured me and Dad suggested that the cowboy needed a girlfriend called Rosepipe. Second, the house in Tait Avenue was the place where one afternoon Tony strapped me to a chair with a saucepan on my head, shut me in an unlit cupboard and, after a suitably formal countdown, told me I was going into space. For ages (it may have been hours or minutes) I sat in that cupboard, content to be orbiting the earth, while Tony, undisturbed, got on with revising for his exams.

But enough about me. Dad's story has reached 1963, he is 41 years old and everyone is wondering if there is a future for a white man in Africa. Because the Federation will wind up at the end of the year, so will the Federal Army. It must have been deeply unsettling, as Dad was happy in the army and by now he had been promoted to Warrant Office Class 1, the highest rank for a non-commissioned officer. There would have been options to transfer to one of the army commands being re-established for each of the separate territories, but I don't know how Dad viewed these at the time. All I can remember, at the end of 1963, was Dad telling us that he was leaving the army and that we were going back to live in England 'forever'. It was to be the family's third return to Britain and it would not be the last 'forever'. It would also be my first journey outside Africa.

An adventure for me, at five years old, it was a familiar groove for Mum, Dad and Stewart. Tony had already left for the UK a few months earlier, to join the Royal Navy. We four took the train to Cape Town and the ship to Southampton. This time it was the RMS Edinburgh Castle and we travelled with another army family, the Cables. There are pictures of dances and parties on board, signifying a sense of celebration which may have been an illusion, masking uncertainties about the future. We arrived in Southampton in the middle of January 1964 and followed the predictable path to Dad's parents in Bexleyheath. Everything – the freezing weather, the people, the food – was strange and fascinating to me. We squashed into the house at 82 Standard Road and there was a round of visits to or from various relatives. Grandparents were wrinkly and a bit scary, perhaps because I had known so few old people in Africa. Tea was drunk and cigarettes were smoked and the grown-ups talked and talked, presumably about serious stuff, job prospects and housing and so on. We visited Tony too, now a Midshipman at the Royal Naval College at Dartmouth.

Very quickly Forever in England turned into Two Months in England. By the end of March we were back on the ship, heading south. Whatever prospects the home country had offered Dad, he had already received a more attractive proposition from the army back in central Africa. While Southern Rhodesia was still considering its political future its former federal partners, Northern Rhodesia and Nyasaland, were scheduled for full independence that same year as the new states of Zambia and Malawi. Determined to avoid the chaos that had followed Belgium's ill-prepared departure from Congo in 1960 the British government was actively supporting the transition, and that would include supplying experienced soldiers to lead and train the armed forces of the new nations. For Dad this meant a promotion, and he was given a choice between Zambia and Malawi. As he and Mum had no experience of the former Nyasaland he chose Zambia, and on the 10th of April 1964 he was commissioned as a Lieutenant in the Army Service Corps, to be based in Lusaka. In a sense, he was coming home.

We were now an officer's family. Rather than live in the barracks, Dad was offered one of the smart bungalows in the Woodlands suburb. It was a period of enormous upheaval in the country. Constitutional changes had led to

Kenneth Kaunda becoming the first black Prime Minister of Northern Rhodesia, on the way to his appointment as President of an independent Zambia in the coming October. Within months his authority as Prime Minister was put to the test, when fighting flared in the north of the country and he was forced to mobilise the army. The origins of the violence lay in the person of Alice 'Lenshina' Mulenga, a self-appointed prophetess and leader of the Lumpa church, a quasi-Christian movement formed by Lenshina after she received a divine revelation – meeting Jesus Christ, so she claimed – during a bout of cerebral malaria in 1953. The church grew to over 150,000 members and by the early sixties it was in direct conflict with Kaunda's UNIP party who were strong in the Lumpa heartland. When violence broke out the government intervened, first with mobile police units and later with armed troops. The months-long conflict was bloody and hundreds of people were killed. Most of the dead were members of the Lumpa church.

As a Service Corps officer Dad wasn't directly involved in any of the fighting but he spent time in Chinsali, the centre of the area of operation where the Northern Rhodesia Regiment set up its base. Dad took colour slides of the activities around the dirt-strip airfield, the comings and goings of the Dakotas bringing supplies from Lusaka. Stewart even managed to hitch a round-trip ride on one of those flights – what harm could a fourteen-year-old come to on a day-trip to a war zone?

The Lumpa uprising, ghastly as it was, raised relatively little concern among the majority of whites. Most of them lived in the cities, in Lusaka or Livingstone or the Copperbelt, far from the troubles. More pressing was their sense of stepping into the unknown as the days counted down towards independence. In spite of assurances by Kaunda that the new Zambia would be a place where white settlers would continue to be welcome, and where their skills and expertise would be needed, many felt that their time was up and they sought a safe haven elsewhere. Where would that place of safety be? Some saw South Africa as the obvious destination; with Apartheid firmly embedded and Nelson Mandela and his fellow troublemakers jailed, the white man looked to be in charge there for a very long time. Southern Rhodesia held similar appeal, although the determination to sustain white rule there would not be formalised until 1965 when the government of Ian Smith declared unilateral independence from Britain. Some returned to Britain – for many 'forever' – and others moved to the USA, Canada, Australia or New Zealand.

For Dad it was a different story. By signing up to the new Zambia Army he had demonstrated his willingness to accept, if not embrace, the new world of black majority rule. And when independence arrived on the 24th October 1964 and we saw the Union Jack replaced by the bright and hopeful colours of the Zambian flag, things looked much the same as they had the day before. Zambia was still a beautiful place with a big, blue sky. Dad was becoming steadily better-off with his officer's salary and treated himself to a second-hand Chevrolet, a cream-coloured machine the size of a small house. I started school and for at least two years my classrooms still saw only white-faced children and teachers. Witnessing a black President reviewing the troops or trivial changes like the Zambianisation of colonial street names was more of a novelty than a cause for concern. Life was good, and the sun continued to shine.

NINE

The year 1965 was a watershed in Dad's position as a white man in Africa. By choosing to live and work in Zambia after independence he had placed himself firmly on one side of a line between the newly independent states and the neighbouring countries which continued to maintain white rule. South Africa looked as if it would hold out indefinitely. Apartheid was established and political opposition neutralised, while a booming economy and the skilled manipulation of foreign interests ensured that the government could uphold white support and resist external pressures for change. The Portuguese colonies of Angola and Moçambique – designated by the mother country as provinces of Portugal - were facing armed opposition from a range of liberation groups funded by communist bloc and western sponsors, but in the mid-sixties the Salazar regime in Lisbon was in no mood to relinquish territories that it had occupied for hundreds of years.

Meanwhile Zambia's closest neighbour, Southern Rhodesia, was carving its own path. UDI, the unilateral declaration of independence declared on the 11th of November 1965, had no precedent in the history of the

British Commonwealth. The architects of UDI sought to play up their continuing allegiance to the Crown and the distinctions between their form of government and the openly racial policies of South Africa. The choice of Armistice Day to declare UDI was no accident, but intended to remind Britain that Southern Rhodesians – now simply 'Rhodesians' – had fought and died side-by side with their British brethren in the two World Wars.

The new Rhodesia, only months earlier a federal partner and economically integrated with Northern Rhodesia, now sat on Zambia's southern border as an ideological enemy. At least, that was the view of the new Zambian government and probably the majority of black Zambians. For the whites in Zambia, the situation was more complex. They had kinsmen in Rhodesia, many of them family members, friends, former colleagues and comrades. It was partly by accident that a man, woman or child found themselves on 'this' or 'that' side of the border, with echoes of the division of Germany after the war. Some in Zambia responded to their allegiances by moving to Rhodesia. Others, perhaps, moved in the other direction. Dad stayed put.

It would be no surprise that the bombshell of UDI raised anxieties within the new Zambian leadership. On one level, they had to come to terms with the new arrangement, recognising that the two countries were still economically co-dependent. But there were security concerns. Zambia had thousands of whites in positions of authority, including the military, who might be loyal to the new regime in Salisbury. Were they a risk to Zambia? Should they be allowed to stay?

Dad, at first, didn't express any concern about his own position in the Zambia Army, but it was clear that the initial welcome extended to those whites willing to support the young country was starting to cool. Aside from any external factors, it would always have been the intention of the Zambian government to 'Zambianise', as quickly as possible, the jobs hitherto held exclusively by whites. Inevitably, and with some justification, many whites believed that this process should be slow and steady. Apart from self-interest – they were in no hurry to give away their livelihood – they recognised the plain fact that the majority of black Zambians had attained only a basic level of education and had a long way to go before they could acquire the knowledge, skills and attitudes to manage the administration and economy of a modern, western style state. In practice the pace of Zambianisation would be a compromise between white interests, practical necessity and the need to satisfy Zambian aspirations.

In the short term none of this affected Dad and his career. At the end of 1965 he was promoted to Captain and during the following year his responsibilities increased, becoming second-in-command and then Acting Officer Commanding of the No. 1 Ordnance and Supply Company of the Zambia Army. He was in charge of the army's supply depot, commanding sixty officers and men and responsible for over £400,000 worth (almost £8 million in today's money) of weapons, ammunition, communications equipment, clothing and food. A reference letter from that period calls him 'a person of high principles and an officer of the greatest integrity ' and 'a very efficient, hardworking and loyal officer with a well-developed sense of responsibility '.

Perhaps I shouldn't speak for my brothers, but I believe that Tony, Stewart and I all hoped that in our different ways we have lived up to that example. In these days when so much is said about the need for boys to have a strong father-figure, a male role-model, I'm grateful that when I was growing up I had Dad to look up to. His loyalty and integrity and his willingness to work hard were as much a part of his family life as they were for his career. In turn, I believe they are a reflection of the stable and loving upbringing which Dad received from his own parents, particularly his mother. I only hope that I have done half as well with my own children, but again, I'm digressing. It is still only 1966, and I'm not yet eight. Dad is forty-four.

If Dad did anything like a mid-life review when he reached that age, I think he would have allowed himself to feel pleased with his achievements. Thirty years earlier he had left school, too young to gain any qualifications, and now he could look back on a respectable piece of war service, a steady marriage and the fathering of three boys. By his own merit he had won an officer rank in the army. He drove the motor car his father had promised he would never own and he had seen more of the world than most of the boys he had grown up with in Bexleyheath. By now both his elder sons had left home and begun their independent lives, Stewart having followed Tony back to England earlier that year. The fact that Tony and Stewart were both in uniform and serving in the Royal Navy attracted a little envy from some of Dad's army friends who yearned to see their own sons follow them into the armed forces.

If the world around him had stood still, taken a rest from the unrelenting march of change, Dad may have been content. But history doesn't work like that. In spite of the outward impression of continuity in the early tranquil months following independence, the pace of change in Zambia was accelerating. United Nations sanctions against the rebels in Salisbury and the Rhodesians' responses to those sanctions were beginning to hurt Zambia. It received many of its goods – including petroleum products - through Rhodesia. The situation led to fuel shortages and for a time the Royal Air Force had to fly petrol directly into Zambia in Bristol Britannia transport aircraft. During the tense early months after UDI Britain needed to demonstrate its resolve in confronting the rebels – in the face of African critics who pressed for direct military action – while keeping the doors open for negotiation. RAF Javelin fighters were symbolically deployed to Zambia, albeit temporarily, and shortly afterwards Britain shouldered a longer-term commitment in the form of the Beira patrol.

Backed up by the UN resolutions authorising sanctions against Rhodesia – but notably placing the burden on Britain - the Beira patrol required the Royal Navy to deploy ships off the coast of Moçambique to intercept tankers approaching the port of Beira and turn away any which might be carrying oil destined for Rhodesia. The patrol went on for nine years; after Portugal relinquished Moçambique as a colony in 1974 Rhodesia lost the support of it neighbour and the patrol lost its raison d'être. Now considered an almost complete failure, the Beira Patrol involved 76 warships and support vessels and cost the British taxpayer around £100 million.

Meanwhile, besides managing the trials imposed on Zambia by the situation in Rhodesia, the new country began to assert its independent-mindedness. While links to Britain remained strong, new friendships were being cultivated. The hand of brotherhood was being extended from a range of new allies - from Belgrade to Moscow, Prague to Peking - as post-colonial Africa offered a chance to extend the reach of Marxism-Leninism. Already steeped in socialist thinking, Zambia's leadership welcomed these overtures, especially if they were sweetened by a package of aid. For Dad the gradual appearance in Zambia of advisors from the wrong side of the Iron Curtain was a sure sign that the country was heading down a rocky path. How long should he stay in the country? With two of his sons now in England, and Tony engaged to be married, perhaps now was the time to make that final, 'forever' journey home to Britain.

By the end the end of 1966 the decision was made and we took that journey. It was my first ride in an aeroplane. True to the times Mum insisted that I should be smartly dressed for the occasion and had me kitted out in a tailor-made suit (my first and last) with short trousers and a jacket bearing my school badge. By today's standards the airport at Lusaka was tiny but it managed to accommodate the BOAC Vickers VC10, a piece of cutting-edge technology, for the flights to and from London. The VC10 was renowned for its tall and graceful tail-plane which towered above our heads as we walked across the tarmac. Straight-faced, Dad pointed it out and explained to Mum that that part of the plane was used as a honeymoon suite. She knew him too well to fall for it.

After eleven hours in that aircraft we touched down bang in the middle of the swinging sixties. Men with long hair − 'they look like girls ' - and afghan coats. Miniskirts. Mini cars. If you had been living in Britain during that decade, these things had crept up on you, step by step. For us, returned from a place whose values and styles sat more comfortably in the forties or fifties, it was a shock. Dad quite liked the miniskirts, I think, but he hated with a vengeance the Rolling Stones - he endlessly parodied in a repetitive monotone the lyric 'Who want's yesterday's papers?', comparing young Jagger with the infinitely superior Sinatra. Mum marvelled at the bright psychedelic colours, the brash confidence of the young people. And we were all a tiny bit dazzled by Tony's fiancé Dinah. She was an air stewardess − in 1966 you couldn't get more glamorous than that − with looks to rival a Shrimpton or a Twiggy. Suddenly Africa seemed a long, long way away.

Because Tony and Stewart were both based in the West Country, Mum and Dad decided that we too should live in that part of England. A bungalow was rented in Exmouth and I was sent to the local primary school, a pretty dire experience which I'll pass over. Dad had to find work, fast, and he fell back on his experience as a showroom assistant to get a job in the electrical department of Exeter's biggest department store, Bobby's. I now think it must have been a knock to his self-esteem. Only months before he had been an army captain with sixty men under him and now he was advising shoppers about different models of vacuum cleaner. I can't imagine it paid very well, either, but beggars can't be choosers. Unknowingly Dad had timed his return to the UK to coincide with a spike in unemployment, which had almost doubled since the previous year.

We stayed in Exmouth for twelve months. During that time I was exposed to an aspect of my parents' lives which was to feature more and more in the years ahead. For the first time I was old enough to tune into their conversations and learn that money – getting it, spending it, keeping it – was a big deal for grown-ups and it was causing my Mum and Dad some heartache. There was talk of trying to buy a house. I clearly remember sitting in the back of the car one afternoon while they discussed a particular property, and hearing Mum say that she didn't want to buy it 'if it means having a mortgage around our necks'. My parents, insulated from economic reality by their years overseas, must have been the only people in Britain – apart from the rich - who hoped buy a house without a mortgage. Yet they had been brought up in the twenties and thirties when thrift was good and debt was bad, so the idea of owing the building society over £2,000, perhaps two or three year's wages, terrified them. What they didn't realise, and they were not the only ones, was that the prosperity of the fifties and sixties was starting to falter and that inflation was taking off. By the early seventies, when Dad next contemplated buying a home, house prices had run far ahead of him. He had saved quite hard in the intervening years, but inflation swallowed up most of the value.

For the whole of her life Mum always dreamed of owning her own home, ideally a nice modern bungalow or a cottage with roses around the door. She even made little drawings of that cottage with coloured pencils. This was inspired, in part, by her two sisters and their husbands becoming home-owners early on in their married lives. They had never left Britain; instead they had led fairly conventional middle-class lives untroubled by adventure.

Mum envied them their homes and their financial security, and Dad bore the brunt of her disappointment. As a child (and as an adult) I felt that this was unfair, because it implied a kind of failure on Dad's part as the family breadwinner. He had always worked hard and rarely spent money on himself. But perhaps there was more to it. Dad certainly wasn't 'good with money' and I'm sure he could have made some smarter choices. Maybe the true source of Mum's grumbling lay elsewhere, in other areas of their relationship or simply within herself. As a child I wouldn't have appreciated these possibilities. I just saw Mum needling Dad in that passive-aggressive way which characterised so many women of her generation. And Dad, like a good soldier, took it on the chin.

I'm not suggesting that our year in Exmouth was all gloom and marital strife. We saw a lot of Stewart and he was invariably good fun. We lived in a pleasant sea-side town and we had trips around the coast, to Dartmoor, to London. Tony and Dinah married, on a gloomy winter's afternoon in Suffolk (tainted by a measure of rancour between the in-laws), and we spent happy family days with them at their cottage in Somerset. My school was dreadful and I made few friends, but I enjoyed the novelty of life in England, playing on the beach, visiting the ice-cream van, kitting out my Action Man and watching TV. One of my favourites was Top of the Pops and Mum and Dad would watch it with me, providing a running commentary on the quality of the music, the appearance of the artists, and their morals. 'That boy's on drugs,' Mum would say, 'look at his eyes.' A few of the popsters met with their approval, the non-druggy ones like Tom Jones who sang a proper tune and even the bare-footed Sandy Shaw, but for Dad the Stones remained firmly out of favour. 'Look at him, ' he would say, 'he's got his back to the audience. When I was on the stage we were told never to turn our back on the audience. Never. '

Viewed from our present decade 1967 is full of

contrasts and similarities. That year saw the UK's application to join the European Economic Community (only to be vetoed, for a second time, by France) and the foundation of the National Front. The first Concorde was rolled out, the QE2 was launched and the Beatles released the Sergeant Pepper's album. There was an outbreak of foot-and-mouth disease. Abortion and homosexuality were decriminalised by a parliament where the ruling Labour party held a strong commons majority. The government had its hands full with a sluggish economy and sharply rising unemployment; the consequent devaluation of the pound was explained by the Prime Minister Harold Wilson with the famous claim that 'It does not mean that the pound here in Britain, in your pocket or purse or in your bank, has been devalued.' On top of all that, Wilson was no nearer to resolving the problem of Rhodesia.

During his time in the UK Dad kept an eye on the goings-on in Africa, both north and south of the Zambezi. In spite of its difficulties Zambia's economy was growing and the young country was attracting plenty of investment. Rather than turn its back on its former territory, Britain was supporting Zambia in the state and private sectors. Workers from Britain were pouring into the Copperbelt, the 'VC-tenners' as they were known, to fill a skills gap and keep the booming copper mines in production. A new generation of government advisors and administrators was moving in too, sometimes jostling for influence with Israelis, Swedes, Americans and Chinese in the post-colonial bun-fight. Many of these public-sector types were hired on fixed-term, well-paid contracts through the Crown Agents, a UK government agency which had been managing overseas recruitment and logistics for centuries.

Dad's details were held on the Crown Agents books, so you can see what's coming. He can't be going back to Africa again? As a child I had no say in the matter. If you are a parent you know how it works; you discuss the serious stuff behind closed doors and, when the decision has been made, you present it to the kids as a *fait accompli*. That was how it was for me at the end of 1967, when Dad told me that we were going back to Zambia. This time he would be a civilian, he explained, working as the Senior Force Armourer for the Zambia Police. The money would be good, apparently, and I guess that was the main reason for Dad accepting the offer. I had no complaints. I was happy to escape from my narrow-minded class-mates and go back to my old school in Lusaka. And more, now I was in the BOAC Junior Jet Club, Dad's latest change of heart would mean extra miles in my log book.

VC10, here we go again.

TEN

I've experienced an unexpected effect of writing about my Dad's past. Immersed day after day in artefacts, events and memories from more than half a century ago I sometimes get the impression, a feeling, that it is all happening now. The past, fleetingly but repetitively, becomes the present. Long-expired family concerns and tensions and national and international crises become real once more. I start to worry about decisions made in 1958 or 1966 or 1973 as if their outcomes still mattered. And because, simultaneously, I already know all the outcomes I suffer from a form of hindsight gloom. Why did they do that? Surely they knew that it would... This sounds silly, I know. The past is the past and there is nothing we can do to change it. But I have reached a stage in Dad's story where I know that some of the choices he made had a profound effect on the direction of my own life – mostly for the good - but not necessarily beneficial for him and Mum.

Back to the present, which means the 8th of October 1967. Dad, Mum and I have said our farewells to family in England – there were few friends, after such a short time - and we have arrived back in Lusaka. I am excited about going back to my old school but I quickly find that my spell of sub-standard education in England has left me more or less a year behind and I have to work hard to catch up. For Mum there is the pleasure of a new house in Birch Road, Woodlands, probably the best home we ever had. She reacquaints with her old friends. Dad gets stuck in to a stimulating and well-paid job and we are all happy to see the sun.

No longer in uniform, Dad goes to work in shirt and tie and semi-casual slacks. Following the trend of the day he even takes up wearing *Veldschoens*, Afrikaner-style suede shoes. I have such clear memories – and plenty of photographs - of Dad from that time. At forty-five he was still a good-looking man, slim and tall with a slightly sun-worn look and near-black hair swept straight back. There is a slight gloss from daily application of Vaseline Hair Tonic, a product I was surprised to find is still on sale today. The hair care, along with the neatly trimmed moustache, hint at a touch of vanity which Dad never tried to conceal. He was proud of the way he looked and he didn't object when people said he looked like David Niven. It wasn't a trait I inherited and when I was a teenager he and Mum despaired of my disinterest in my appearance, equating it with a lack of self-respect.

I also remember Dad's workplace. He had a spacious office, sometimes shared with a clerk, attached to the Zambia Police armourer's workshop. There were venetian blinds on the metal-framed windows to keep out the glare of the sun, but no fans or air conditioning. In those days I think that air conditioning was seen as something for pansies, or Americans. The workshop itself was a big square space filled with rows of work-benches, each equipped with vices and hand-tools for servicing and repairing the weapons. On the opposite side to the office was the blueing room, a place of noxious smells, and a secure, multi-padlocked store for the guns themselves. Rows of rifles secured with chains through their trigger-guards. Everywhere the aroma of linseed oil. Dad's team of armourers were all Zambian policemen and although I can't recall their names – apart from the man who would succeed Dad, Inspector Shula – I remember that I got to know them quite well. I regularly spent afternoons at the workshop after school (lessons finished at one o'clock) and I developed a fascination for guns.

One of the tasks which Dad had to manage was the destruction of weapons that had been confiscated by, or surrendered to the police. At least once every year or two a huge haul, collected from all over Zambia, was delivered to the workshop. If you are a modern-day collector of vintage weapons you would have drooled over the great metallic pile which appeared on the workshop floor. World War II Luger and Mauser pistols. Shotguns of various bores and configurations. A multitude of revolvers: Webley, Smith and Wesson, Colt. Automatic pistols from the dainty to the macho. My favourite was an enormous home-made flint-lock weapon with a smooth-bore barrel, mounted on a decoratively carved wooden stock, fashioned from a heavy-duty piece of pipe. Allegedly it had been used for shooting elephants.

If a firearm looked serviceable Dad might allow the letting off of a few rounds in the indoor test-firing range before the confiscated item was destroyed. He had organised the building of the range, a long low building made out of reinforced concrete panels. One day, while the roof of the range at the target end was still unfinished, Dad took a Heckler and Koch G3 assault rifle into the range to test it. I don't know who did the actual firing – it might have been Dad himself - but his aim wasn't as good as it might have been and a number of rounds went high, through the gap where the roof should be, and arrived several hundred yards away on the other side of a main road. No-one was hurt, but a window in the Caterpillar tractor depot was broken and the embarrassed Senior Force Armourer had to apologise on behalf of the Zambia Police. I guess someone in Caterpillar kept the bullet as a souvenir.

Responsibility for the destruction of confiscated weapons exposed Dad to his first taste of corruption in high places. A government minister, someone quite senior who Dad would not name, got wind of the fact that these weapons were being brought to Lusaka and that many of them were serviceable and desirable pieces. The gentleman telephoned Dad and asked if he could buy them, something he would have known was illegal. Dad politely declined the offer and nothing more was heard of it, but it was a small sign of things to come for poor Zambia. More positively, Dad was pressing on with the key task assigned to him: to train up the team of Zambian armourers and to identify and prepare his successor. He sent away the three or four most able police armourers for advanced training with the British Army in the UK, a unique experience for men who had never before left Zambia. When we had a family holiday back in England in 1970 we paid them a surprise visit at Bordon Camp in Hampshire. I remember a cold and misty afternoon – I think it was a Sunday, a day off – and they emerged from their barrack hut with blankets wrapped around their shoulders, sleepy-eyed. Once they saw Dad and realised why their Sunday rest had been disturbed, their faces brightened, there was vigorous hand-shaking all round and they began to tell us about their recent adventures.

For some reason the only thing I remember the policemen saying, perhaps because Dad repeated it later, was that they were terribly shocked by British television. To the Zambians it seemed incredible that people on TV like political commentators and comedians - they singled out the impersonator Mike Yarwood - were permitted to make fun of the Prime Minister. Nothing of the sort would have been allowed on Zambian TV. By 1970 Kenneth Kaunda had consolidated his grip on power, having banned all the opposition parties and embarked on the creation of a personality cult wrapped up in 'African

Socialism' and 'Zambian Humanism'. Six years after independence the concepts of parliamentary democracy inherited from the colonial master were being moulded into a new image.

***

When I look at our family photo albums, or project the slides which Dad took with his new Yashica camera during that golden time between 1967 and 1970, things look pretty damned good. Perhaps the shift from monochrome to colour has something to do with it. Mum in pretty sleeveless dresses showing off her brown arms, the hemlines now migrated above the knee. Grown-up parties and outings with my parents' friends. My own barefooted self grinning beside my Mum and our dog Barney in the garden which Mum nurtured in Birch Road. Dad and his male friends, now mainly civilians, chatting, smoking, all wearing white shirts and ties (mostly regimental) for a weekend get-together.

There is one picture of Dad in masonic regalia. Over his dinner jacket (surprisingly for Dad, his bow-tie is slightly crooked) he is wearing a long pointy collar thing and around his waist is an apron. I remember the look and feel of those items. They were magnificently crafted and adorned with little emblems whose meaning only a freemason could explain. On either side of the apron was a set of tiny silver balls hanging on chains which always made me think of those swinging ball desk toys which were fashionable at the time. This masonic ensemble, which was unique to Dad's lodge in Lusaka, was exquisitely hand-made in pale blue silk and it must have cost a bomb.

For a man who never had hobbies or joined clubs or societies it was quite a turning point for Dad to be invited to join the masons. For Mum and me it was a novelty, what with the strange get-up and all the secrecy. 'It's not a secret society, ' Dad would say, 'It's a society with secrets.

' Mum would tease him about it - gently - but I think she was happy to see him go to his lodge and enjoy some of the male camaraderie which perhaps he had lost when he left the army. In a sense, the masons were putting him back in uniform, and it was good for him. I also believe that the simple fact of being invited to join, of being chosen, mattered a lot to Dad. For all his breezy humour and apparent self-confidence Dad needed affirmation, recognition of his value. Don't we all? He received that recognition through his inclusion in an opaque but apparently influential group within Lusaka's little social scene.

What went on at Dad's lodge meetings on a Thursday evening I will never know. There were rituals and promises, some complicated stuff that Dad had to memorise from a little book, and there was business related to the charitable works which masons perform as their service to the community. I think that is all common knowledge. But beyond that I have never tried to find out. Somehow, even fifty years later, it would feel disrespectful towards Dad and his 'society with secrets' to go prying where I'm not wanted. While on the one hand, as an adult, I look at the whole masonic thing as a bit weird and potentially subversive, my stronger instinct is to show respect for something which meant a great deal to my Dad at the time.

All this takes us away from the onward march of events in Zambia. Dad and his family may have been living in a comfortable bubble but throughout the sixties he had already seen more change than most people could have imagined and he knew it wasn't going to stop. By the end of the decade President Kaunda's brand of socialism delivered two big shifts – nationalisation of many of Zambia's industries and the accelerated 'Africanisation' of the workforce – which were intended to channel the rewards of capital towards the nation's development and help equalise opportunity. Well-intentioned perhaps, but ill-managed on both fronts, these measures led to decades of economic decline, inflation, shortages of goods and poverty for many of Zambia's citizens. Not that the government can take all the blame; factors outside its control like falling copper prices and the rising cost of oil were to play a big part in the story, but for expatriates like my Mum and Dad it began to cast a dark shadow over their future. No longer could they realistically imagine staying in Africa for the rest of their lives.

In defence of poor Zambia and its sometimes incompetent and corrupt leaders, it did a lot better than many other young African nations in the years to come. It avoided the violence we associate with Congo, Angola, Zimbabwe and many others in a long, sad list. It never had a rapacious monster like Idi Amin, Charles Taylor, Omar Al-Bashir or Robert Mugabe at the helm. Yet Dad wasn't to know, back in the late 1960's that Zambia might not suddenly spiral out of control like one of its neighbours. At the time the horrors of the civil war over Katanga were still fresh in people's memories.

**

1970 was a year we all remembered. Dad had earned several months of paid leave and free return flights home (meaning England) for his family. By the start of the year I already had a place at boarding school in the UK, to start in the September, so Mum and Dad agreed that it would be OK for me to skip the final term at junior school. Dad was absorbed with fulfilling a lifelong dream to buy his first brand-new car. The car, an Opel Rekord estate, was ordered in advance and would be handed over to Dad when we arrived at Heathrow. I can't exaggerate how much that car meant to Dad. For months before our trip we would make almost weekly trips to the Opel showroom in Lusaka, just to look at the cars and touch them and smell the new upholstery. There was much deliberation about the model to choose, and the colour. It had to be a

German car – Dad always admired the Germans – but he couldn't afford a Mercedes so the Opel was a good bet at around £800. He would have liked metallic paint but that was a bit pricy so he chose a conservative dark blue. I'm not sure why we needed an estate instead of a saloon.

We flew to London in April, met at the airport by Tony and Dinah with their little daughter Samantha and Stewart with his fiancé Heather. Dad collected the Opel and it was admired by all. A bungalow was rented in Devon and we began the usual round of visits to relatives and friends and trips to the seaside. It was all very relaxed. In the run-up to the holiday Mum had had surgery, a hysterectomy. Not that I was told why she was in hospital – each day Dad just took me to see her, and with all the tubes and fluids and medical paraphernalia I assumed she was dying and took myself off to wander around the grounds, fighting off the tears. By the time we got to England, the episode was almost forgotten.

During that summer Mum and Dad took me to visit my school-to-be, which was pretty exciting, and forked out a fortune for the uniform. It was all very Tom Brown's Schooldays (which I read that year) but I never did wear those cricket whites. My expensive English schooling was to be another perk of Dad's job and it would include free flights home for the holidays – I would become a VC-tenner in my own right. But during that endless summer (I know that's a cliché but small boys always remember 'endless summers') school was a long way off and our family was enjoying, for the first time in many years, the five of us being together in the same part of the world. There was also the added novelty (and considerable emotional adjustment, for Mum) of an extended family - Tony married with one child and another on the way, and Stewart close to tying the knot with Heather.

Of course the summer wasn't endless, they never are. By the middle of July it was time for Dad to have his precious car loaded into the hold of the Royal Mail Ship

Windsor Castle and for us all to board the liner at Southampton for the voyage back to Africa. It had been more than six years since we had travelled by sea and the ship was faster and more modern than the last one, taking only eleven days to reach Cape Town. I'm sure Mum and Dad enjoyed the touch of luxury and apart from a day of seasickness I was fairly content. In Cape Town the Opel was retrieved – without a scratch – and we set off along the coast of South Africa, enjoying the magnificent scenery of the Garden Route and stopping off for a week in Durban where we could enjoy the dubious privilege of swimming from a whites-only beach. After eleven days on the road we crossed the border into Rhodesia. From that point Dad must have been hell-bent on getting home to Zambia because, according to the stamps in his passport, we arrived at the Zambian border near Livingstone the following day – a five hundred mile drive. I remember those hours, driving through the night, and the baby baboon which Dad ran over when the poor animal tried to cross the road. Lucky it wasn't a big one, or it might have damaged the new car.

Back in Lusaka (after another day's drive, although I think we rested first for a day or two in Livingstone), life went back to normal. Except it didn't, really. Dad was back to work and I briefly went back to school, rather disappointed that my schoolmates hadn't missed me, or even noticed that I had been away for three months. But September was getting closer, and the fantasy of boarding school had become the reality of leaving home and not seeing my Mum and Dad for twelve weeks. On the outside, at first, I was still chirpy Tim while Mum and Dad were full of smiles and practical advice. On the inside I was in a fog of confused feelings which led, until I finally stepped on to the plane, to a state of depression. That's my adult diagnosis, by the way. Back then I was just plain miserable and my thoughts and feelings were inexplicably detached from any concrete anxiety about leaving home.

Predictably Mum over-reacted and just made me feel worse. Equally predictable, Dad was quietly supportive.

This is Dad's story so I apologise for talking about my eleven-year-old self. And I'm sorry – a bit - for taking a pot-shot at Mum. Much later, looking back, I came to understand that she was probably suffering more than I was. At the age of forty-seven, with two mastectomies and a hysterectomy behind her, she was just about to wave goodbye to her youngest child. What was she going to do with herself? She didn't have a job, she couldn't drive a car and while she was mightily house-proud and enjoyed pottering in the garden, she hardly had a full diary. Even the housework was mostly done by a servant. We can only guess what Dad made of his wife's situation. By nature he always hoped for the best and kept things light and cheery. Over the coming months and years his optimism would be put to the test.

Lusaka, 1964. Driving a desk in a new army.

Lusaka, 1965. A rare burst of physical exertion.

Zambia Police, 1968.

Changing times. Cocktail party at Zambia Police
Headquarters, around 1970.

ELEVEN

As it turned out boarding school wasn't so bad so we can forget about me, at least for the time being. From late in 1970 until early 1973 Mum and Dad were on their own in term-time. While I was away at school I got news from home through letters, which were usually written by Dad. I still have the first one he sent me, which was accompanied by a parcel of edibles – I had learned to call it 'tuck' - to help me settle in. Dad signed off the letter with a PS: 'Barney says Wuff Wuff '.

Those letters were light, newsy, and anecdotal. There was no hint of any difficulties at home, so it would be many years before I learned what a rough time Mum went through when her house became childless after twenty-five years. When I did go home for the holidays I could see that Mum was changing, becoming more and more complaining, but I put that down to the downhill slide in living conditions in Zambia. There was plenty to grumble about, not least the growing number of burglaries which left the better-off, mostly expatriate families feeling increasingly insecure. In truth, life was still very comfortable when you compare it with the hardships that Zambians would suffer in the eighties and nineties, but for my parents it contrasted sharply with the tranquility of their earlier African years.

While Dad was still enjoying his work, attending his lodge, and each morning the reliable Zambian sun continued to shine, there was no longer any question about a permanent move back to the UK – it was now a matter of when. Stewart was married and soon more grandchildren were on their way, so there was an even stronger tug to the home country. Mum fantasised about her rose-draped cottage and Dad did his best to save up for it. I don't know how closely Dad was following events in Britain during that time; because we didn't have a short-wave radio in our house there was no BBC World Service and there wasn't much political analysis in those week-old copies of the News of the World. So he may not have realised just how fast things were changing.

Dad kindled in me an early interest in politics when, during our holiday in England in 1970, the two of us had stayed up on the night of the 18th of June to follow the results of the general election on TV. Ted Heath's Conservatives were not expected to triumph that night but they emerged victorious, winning a comfortable majority which Theresa May would have died for. Dad was pleased. Heath, the yachtsman, musician, sophisticate and ambiguous bachelor cast a sharp contrast to his predecessor, the pipe-smoking family man Harold Wilson. We now know, of course, that the wily Wilson was down but not out – he was back in No 10 in 1974. We also know that whichever party was in power during the 1970's they would have a devil of a job on their hands. Such is the privilege of hindsight.

Sadly for Heath & Co (and for Dad, come to think of it) they were living in the moment and had no crystal ball to reveal the full magnitude of the changes that were going to shape Britain and the world during that troubled decade. Almost continuously, from the end the Second World War until that year of Heath's victory, the British people had enjoyed a rising standard of living, low inflation and almost full employment. No wonder they didn't care about losing the Empire. Whoever held power, Labour or Tory, life was much the same. From time to time the government would tweak the levers to keep the economy growing, pumping in cash from borrowing or taxation, and somehow it seemed to work. The magic – manipulating what economists called the multiplier effect (dreamt up by their guru John Maynard Keynes back in the thirties and forties) - looked like it would go on working forever. Regrettably, it didn't.

A new word came into the politician's vocabulary: stagflation. The unhappy pairing of stagnant growth and rising inflation became the norm during the 1970's. Unemployment rose. Workers who saw the value of their pay packets swallowed up by inflation (already over 6% when Heath won his first election, almost 25% by 1975) had to push for higher and higher wages. If they were backed by one of the big unions their claims were often won; this further stoked up prices in a self-defeating spiral. Strikes and works-to-rule became the order of the day, bludgeoning industrial output and earning the country its label as the Sick Man of Europe. As if the government didn't have enough on its plate, it also had to handle the shock of 1973 when the major oil producing countries embargoed sales to much of the western world, trebling the price of oil. Meanwhile, a civil war was breaking out in Northern Ireland; by the end of 1974 almost a thousand people had lost their lives and there would be many more.

This was the Britain that Dad decided he would return to from sunny Africa. Paradoxically, Britain in decline wasn't necessarily unhappy Britain. For those affected by the conflict in Northern Ireland or for the men and women who lost their jobs it was a grim time, but for many the 1970's are the years of happy memories. The power cuts and the petrol shortages and the three-day-weeks were endured with a Dunkirk spirit. Unfortunately for Mum and Dad, there was one feature of those years of crisis which couldn't be shrugged off with a smile.

Price inflation, the rising cost of food, clothing, petrol and so on; it also meant inflation in the price of homes. Dad must have thought about this, as he was hoping to return to England and buy his first house, but he didn't grasp the scale of problem. In the end, for a variety of reasons, he made up his mind to leave Africa for the last time in 1973. Since his previous visit to England annual inflation had climbed to about 9%, but over the same period the price of an average house had doubled. Those hard-earned savings which Dad had squirreled away, the nest-egg he put aside to buy Mum her little dream cottage or seaside bungalow suddenly looked pretty meagre. It was a nasty blow.

You might think that Dad could still have taken out a mortgage and bought a house with his savings as a substantial deposit. On his return to the UK he had found work quite quickly as a buyer with Mendip District Council in Somerset. A job in local government looked secure. Against this background I don't know why Dad didn't try to borrow the money for a house, given that being a home-owner would mean so much to him, and even more to Mum. It may have had something to do with their old-fashioned aversion to debt (something that the rest of Britain had long since abandoned), or it might have been that the numbers didn't add up. Perhaps Dad wasn't earning enough to get a mortgage. What I do know is that by leaving Zambia Dad had relinquished the benefit of his employer paying my school fees. Those fees, albeit subject to a small subsidy from the County Council, would be a huge burden on my parents' finances for the next four years.

I didn't have to stay on at an expensive private school. I was doing well enough academically for Mum and Dad to conclude that I could manage quite adequately at the local comprehensive. So why did they allow me to stay on, swallowing up their savings? It might be that after three years in that cosseted environment they thought I had become too much of a toff to survive in the real world. I mentioned this to my Uncle Ron when I saw him last year. He told me that my success at school meant a great deal to my Dad; because of that he was more than happy to make the sacrifice, thinking that he was giving his son the best education possible. I hope, in later years, that Mum and Dad still thought it was worth it.

Unable to buy their own house, Mum and Dad lived in council houses for the rest of their lives. I remember three different houses, in Street and Wells in Somerset. They were all comfortable homes in nice-enough neighbourhoods with adequate space for a family of three (becoming two when I left home in 1977). They each had small gardens where Dad, for the first time in his life, started to kindle an interest in growing things. In Africa Mum had protested that Dad never showed any enthusiasm for her gardening projects, but now he was getting stuck in with spade and trowel and seedlings. He missed Zambia and its climate and he missed the open and relaxed social life from his African days, but there were compensations, not least having his children and grandchildren close by. Although I continued boarding my school was only an hour or so from home, thanks to the M5 motorway which had recently been extended into the West Country. Tony and Stewart and their families were also nearby, and Mum and Dad loved being grandparents. By the time they returned to England there were four little ones to dote over, Samantha, Rebecca, Kelvin and Emma. It was painful for them when Tony and Dinah divorced.

Mum had returned to the UK in 1972. She had travelled in advance of Dad to spend time with her sister Pat, who was terminally ill. As I remember it, from that year onwards and throughout my teenage and early adult years, she was at a low ebb. In Zambia she had grumbled about Zambia. In England she grumbled about England.

She sniped at Dad about having to live in a council house. She missed her friends. And she became almost obsessive towards Tony; mother and eldest son became locked in a weird love-hate relationship which drove me – and presumably Dad – crackers. Through it all Dad stayed loyal and calm and supportive. He loved Mum and, equally, he wanted a quiet life.

I know this all paints Mum in a poor light and over the years since she died I have tried to understand why she was so troubled and unhappy while Dad managed to stay, or at least appear, so positive and cheerful. Mum never had the benefit of counselling; her only therapy later in life was the daily Valium which the NHS doled out so freely in those days. So she didn't get a chance to examine herself, to reflect and understand and – above all – to be listened to. As I've said before, she was the product of her generation, a subordinate female in a family of males. It was no wonder she always wished for a daughter.

One day, when Mum was already in her sixties, she asked me out of the blue if 'I ever knew she had been in Chainama '. I knew what she meant, although I hadn't heard the word for ten or twenty years. Chainama meant the Chainama Hills Mental Hospital in Lusaka. Mum explained that sometime in the early seventies, while I was away at school, she had become so depressed - to the extent of refusing to leave her bed for days on end - that she had been admitted to that institution as an in-patient. Dad had never told me about it, at the time or later. I can't remember how long Mum said she stayed in the hospital; it was probably no more than a few weeks and I guess Dad was allowed to visit her from time to time. She said that there had been a young Zambian girl there, a teenager or young adult who was a permanent resident. She formed an attachment to Mum and took to sleeping on the floor under Mum's bed every night. She cadged cigarettes off Mum and for a time they became friends, of a sort. Apart from that, Mum never told me anything about that episode in her life. I don't even know what treatment, if any, she received. Perhaps sharing her cigarettes with that unfortunate young woman, someone who was in the same boat, might have served as a kind of therapy.

After she told me this story Mum asked me if I was ashamed of her, because she had been in an asylum. I told her I wasn't, and wondered why it had taken her so long to tell me.

***

Through it all, Dad plodded on. There were to be no more new cars, no proper holidays – sometimes he struggled to pay the electricity bill. Briefly, I think it was in 1975 or 1976, he tried to return to Zambia. A job was advertised, his CV matched the profile, and he passed the interview at the Crown Agents in London. But the Zambian government wouldn't give him a work permit. He had served their country with loyalty and integrity for more than a decade, but his face no longer fitted. He did a good job hiding his disappointment and went back to his gardening. He still had his family to keep him occupied and the grandchildren brought him more and more pleasure as they got older. In turn they thought he was hilarious and still swap stories about him now.

Time passed. Governments came and went. I left home. Tony had a girlfriend, a nursing sister called Annie, and in due course they married and eventually produced another grandchild, Tom. All these things caused their measure of turbulence or joy. Dad read letters from friends in Africa and listened to the news and saw how irreversibly his old world had past. Month by month, in spite of his well-concealed worries about Mum, he began to adjust to his new life. He enjoyed small pleasures, like The Two Ronnies and The Good Life. Tinned prawns with white bread and butter on a Sunday evening. He wore a tie – weekday or weekend – and stayed teetotal. He experimented with a beard; it didn't suit him. He tried to give up smoking, which suited him even less. He read the Daily Mail and listened to Radio 4. And he drove his little Morris 1100, LGJ 592K, ignoring the fact that he had been in Britain for several years and still hadn't got around to obtaining a driving licence. He eventually sorted that out, after a disheartening series of test attempts, in the next decade.

The end of the seventies, as we all know, was the start of Thatcher. On polling day in 1979 I was twenty years old and Dad was fifty-seven. Dad voted for the party led by lady with the blue eyes and the handbag, and so did I.

But I'm guessing that Mum didn't vote with her husband - she always hated Mrs T.

TWELVE

If you are old enough, the nineteen-eighties can feel like the day before yesterday. In reality, those years are more than a generation behind us. If we look back from 2019 to 1982 it is the same as viewing 1945 from 1982.

I can't remember where I was on New Year's Eve, when 1980 arrived. I wasn't at home, but I know Mum and Dad would have stayed up until midnight to see in the new decade. It was something they always did, even if no-one else was there. They would wait for Big Ben to strike on the TV and kiss one another and say Happy New Year. In younger days there had been parties and dressing up, whether it was a regimental do in the colonial days or, later, a night out at a smart hotel in Lusaka. When the previous decade opened I had even been invited join them and their grown-up friends (there are pictures to prove it) and it all seemed terribly sophisticated; I was twelve and I hit the dance floor, without protest, in my school uniform. Now, approaching their sixties, my parents' social life was almost non-existent.

By now they were settled in Wells, in Somerset. It's a pretty place, quiet and historic, a gentle corner of the country, yet somehow Mum and Dad never made many friends there. There were acquaintances with neighbours; a pair of elderly spinsters, daughters of a former Governor of Nyasaland, enjoyed meeting fellow colonials. Dad got on well with the retired postman who lived next-door-but-one. They shared the odd cup of tea, but never much more. After Africa, where the expatriate scene throws up a ready-made circle of friends, it was a bit dull and a bit lonely. Dad rubbed along well enough with his work colleagues, but most of them were much younger and he never met them outside the office. Mum wasn't working and she never had the confidence to join any clubs or societies, so her opportunities to meet new people were almost zero.

I remember asking Dad around that time why he didn't try to hook up with the local freemasons. I always thought that the whole point of being a mason (or a Rotarian or a Round-Tabler or whatever) was that you belonged; it placed you on the inside of a group where people – men – offered one another support and friendship. Networking, mutual back-scratching. In answer to my question Dad was non-committal, evasive, so I didn't push it. I already had a theory about why he didn't attempt to join a masonic lodge when he returned to England. I think it was all to do with class, or money, or both. In Zambia Dad had been nearer the top of the social ladder (having a white skin automatically pushed you up a few rungs, anyway) and he had more cash in his pocket. In the home country I think Dad imagined he would be a poor cousin among influential masons with posher accents, smarter cars and better connections. If that's true, it's a pity, because in reality Dad might have been welcomed with open arms and his life, and Mum's, would have been richer for it.

Incidentally, I think another activity that Dad could have taken up was writing. He had always written fluent and professional letters; his friend Bill Young in Lusaka had first turned to Dad when he needed someone to craft an urgent letter, to be passed to a Zambian government minister, in an effort to avoid Bill's imminent deportation. Dad's letter proved sufficiently persuasive and Bill was allowed to stay in the country. Dad's work, writing formal reports and the like, had sharpened his skills over the years. At the beginning of 1973, when he was alone in Zambia while Mum was in England with her sister, he had filled his time by writing a novel. Over and over I asked to read it, but Mum wouldn't let me. She said that the story was too much like their early years of marriage. In due course she threw away the type-written manuscript and poor Dad was put off any further literary effort.

Not that it was all boredom. True, Mum continued to suffer from depression but she did her best to fill her days, keeping an immaculate house, feeding Dad, washing his clothes and hosting a string of visiting offspring and grandchildren. She enjoyed drawing and painting and tapestries. She and Dad followed my life and the lives of my brothers and their families with interest, support and love. Our photographs were displayed with pride around the house – especially the one with Stewart and the Prince of Wales.

Stewart was a helicopter aircrewman in the Royal Navy and he had been selected to fly with the Prince a few years earlier. Now, like his older brother, he was considering the move to Civvie Street. During almost twenty years in the service of the Queen Stewart had put in an enormous amount of sea time and he was ready for a proper home life with his family. By early 1982 the days were counting down to his final break from the Senior Service, and he was looking forward to hanging up the blue suit and growing his hair.

Meanwhile, up in London, the Prime Minister was up to her pearl-studded ears in it. By now her government had served up some of the strong economic medicine which she became so famous for, but the Sick Man of Europe was refusing to recover. Inflation stayed doggedly high and unemployment had rocketed to that eye-watering figure, which some of us will remember, of three million. She was also fighting battles within her Tory ranks – at least some things don't change – and she looked far from the invincible figure of later mythology. Simultaneously, 7,000 miles from Downing Street, another leader was struggling to keep his country in order. A place of repression, torture and a collapsing economy, Leopoldo Galtieri's Argentina needed something to distract the people and boost the President's popularity. So in the spring of 1982 he ordered the invasion of the Falkland Islands, a British territory in the South Atlantic over which the Argentines had harboured a claim for 150 years.

We all know how Mrs Thatcher mobilised the armed forces and launched that task force which ejected the Argies and raised the Union Jack at Port Stanley on the 14th of June. Instead of drifting comfortably into civilian life, Stewart was called to play his part in our enemy's defeat. He was in the thick of it; as an experienced aircrewman he was posted to a hurriedly assembled commando helicopter squadron which sailed south and supported the men who fought their way across the islands during that southern winter. On his return Stewart made me smile when he said that it had been an awful long way to go to save a place that looked like Dartmoor, but while he was still down there we were all worried sick. As we followed the news, day by day and night by night, we knew that there was always a chance he might not come back.

Dad had seen war; he was under no illusions about this new one but he hoped that it would all be over quickly (it was, at a price of over 900 human lives) and that Stewart would come home safe. Mum too had her own memories of war, and she suffered as only a mother can, her pain channeled into deep loathing for That Woman who had sent her son off to fight a stupid war in a place that most of us had never heard of. I made inept attempts to boost her spirits which make me cringe now I remember them. In the end only one thing mattered – luck was on Stewart's side and he returned from the Falklands without a scratch. We had a little party, and I have a picture of Dad hanging a home-made medal, an oversized wooden star, around Stewart's neck.

Family life, placed on hold for those long months of the conflict, went back to normal. Dad was now sixty and beginning to think about retirement. I'm not sure why, because money was still tight and his work wasn't all that taxing, but in 1985, at sixty-three, he decided to accept a tiny severance package and take things easy. There was a small pension and he looked forward to a top-up from the state when he reached sixty-five. That birthday came around quickly – they do, at that age – and poor Dad had a nasty surprise. Because he had been abroad for most of his working life, there had been about twenty-five years when he hadn't been paying national insurance contributions. He hadn't realised, and nobody had told him, how much this would reduce his state pension. Staring ahead towards old age, things didn't look too bright. For a while, to make ends meet, Dad took a part-time job as an attendant at a run-down filling station. It was in a wind-swept spot a few miles out of town, damp and exposed in the winter months. It was a long way from Africa.

These days – it was much the same thirty years ago - most people hold out the hope that they will live to a ripe age, eighty-something or maybe more. This year, 2019, more than 14,000 people in the UK are over a hundred. The statistics of increasing life expectancy support an optimism which is tempered by the quiet fear of infirmity or senility which those later years might also bring. I know I used to worry when I imagined Dad or Mum in their eighties or nineties. I thought that we three brothers would have to share a burden of responsibility for our parents' care in their declining years. In truth, my anxieties were misplaced. Within four years of Dad's retirement he had lost the love of his life - our Mum - and his own years were nearing an end.

Mum died at the age of sixty-six, on the 11th of June 1989. A few days earlier she had spent a night in hospital for some tests, as preparation for a long-expected repair to a hiatus hernia, and she was supposed to return to the same hospital for the actual operation within the week. By then I had been married a couple of years and I called in with Jude, my six-months-pregnant wife, to see Mum during her first hospital visit. She seemed bright, a little anxious about the operation but hopeful that it would give her some relief from the pain she had been suffering for many years. We amused her and Dad with a story from our journey; for some reason we had been driving home to Manchester from Jude's parents in Wales with a pair of Burmese cats in the boot of our car. When we arrived at the hospital in Bristol, we found that both cats had had diarrhoea – caused by the stress of the journey, we assumed - and the insides of their cage and the floor of the car's boot were... well, you can imagine it.

We didn't stay long. We kissed Mum goodbye and wished her all the best for the operation. Dad took her home. Within a day she began to feel ill, with chest pains which she and Dad probably assumed were caused by the intrusive prodding and probing of the previous day's medical tests. But Dad took no chances, he rang for an ambulance and Mum was hurried back to the hospital. That night he rang me to say that Mum was unwell and that I should come down. I hesitated; she couldn't be all that bad, surely. He pressed the point, and I understood. Mum had had a heart attack and her condition was not good.

The same day we drove back to Bristol and saw Mum once more in a hospital bed. I'm sure Stewart and Heather were there, probably Tony and Annie too, but I can't clearly remember. Mum looked tiny and grey-skinned in her nightie – I'm no medic but I could see she was really ill. And she kept being sick. But she was pleased to see us, resting her hand on the neat round bump of Jude's tummy and telling her to 'look after that baby '. I moved away to speak to one of the nurses and I saw that he had tears in his eyes. He told me as gently as he could that Mum might not survive the night. I was shocked and puzzled. She was in a hospital, in the cardiac unit, for heaven's sake. Surely they could fix whatever was wrong with our Mum.

Eventually we went home, back to Wells with Dad and Stewart and Heather. Very early the next morning Dad had a call from the hospital to say that Mum had had another cardiac arrest. We went back to the hospital together and by the time we arrived she had died. The next time I saw her was in the chapel of rest at the undertaker's. I had never seen a dead person before. Dad had spent some time in there, alone with the body of his beloved wife, and then he left and Tony, Stewart and I took our turn as a threesome. The funeral people had done a professional job; Mum's face was made up, they had smoothed the lines and her hair was bright and glossy. The three of us looked at each other, stumbling to find things to say. I leaned over the coffin and kissed Mum goodbye – I had seen someone do it once, on TV - and I was repelled by the rigidity, the coldness of death. I will never repeat that experience. A body was there but Mum was gone, forever.

There was a cremation and we had a gathering of family and friends. Dad was Dad, warm and welcoming to the mourners, but in a diminished version of his usual self. We brothers and our spouses did what we could with the arrangements, and Jude and I stayed on with Dad for a couple of days. When we finally left him alone in the house he kissed me – a rare thing for our family – and we left him with promises to come back soon. I remember the stale smell of Dad's misery; he had neglected to have a bath. Jude and I went back to work and carried on getting things ready for the new baby. I can't imagine how it was for Dad, to be left alone in the house on that bright summer evening. Just before we left, I asked if he wanted any help getting rid of Mum's clothes. The suggestion was so crass that he should have ejected me from the house, but instead he gently explained that it was much too soon for all that.

For many years Mum had had frequent spells of ill health so Dad was used to fending for himself. He could cook basic meals, wash and iron the laundry and keep the house tidy, although the hoovering and dusting and polishing would never match Mum's standards. Things like bills and paperwork had always been his affair anyway. His routines, without Mum, were not much changed. He took turns visiting his sons and their families, sometimes staying with us for two or three weeks at a stretch. Jude did her best to feed him up; he lost a lot of weight after Mum died. Dad was only sixty-seven but he rapidly began to look like a very old man, his collars too big and his clothes drooping from his shoulders.

1989. It's thirty years past, as I write this. The Berlin Wall came down and the Cold War, the backdrop to most of Dad's adult life, showed signs of nearing its end. Chinese protesters were shot down by troops in Tiananmen Square. The white leaders of South Africa, the descendants of the Nationalists who had entered government when Dad first moved there forty years earlier, were offering a tentative olive branch to Nelson Mandela. At Deal Barracks in Kent, where Dad had seen out the end of his wartime service, an IRA bomb killed eleven young Royal Marines.

Those public milestones, transient images from the TV news, are blanketed out by private memory of events closer to home. Dad had lost his wife of forty-six years and it is no exaggeration to say he was crushed. But soon we would have a piece of good news to soothe his grief. On the 8th of October Jude produced our first child, a son. Alexander – Alex – was Dad's sixth grandchild, a gift to us all just when we needed it but the elation generated by his arrival was short-lived. At the end of October Tony telephoned Dad to say that his daughter Rebecca, nineteen years old, had been killed in a car accident in Lincolnshire along with her fiancé Barry.

***

Dad saw just one blessing in this, the darkest episode in our family's life. At least, he said, Mum hadn't had to experience the premature death of her beautiful granddaughter. Only recently she had lived through the fear of losing a son, when Tony suffered a brain haemorrhage. By now Tony was well on the road to recovery, and he was to live another ten years before the same affliction returned to strike him down for good. By then, 1999, Dad was gone too, so neither of our parents had to live through the loss of their first-born child.

It is hard to estimate the effect of Rebecca's accident (such an innocent word, accident) upon Dad. Another decade came along and he withered. Above all, he was lonely. When he came to visit us, having driven his Fiesta up what he called the Pensioner's Lane of the M5 and M6, he would hurry out of the car with his arms already reaching out, ready to scoop up baby Alex and squeeze him and kiss him. Alex, a little scrap of new life in Dad's world, was a connection with Mum. When Jude felt low or inadequate as a brand-new mother, Dad reassured. His body was fading, he was no longer the strong and capable man I remembered from my childhood, but he still had love and he wanted to share it.

Dad hung on to life for another three years. Fifty years of smoking rapidly caught up with him and his lungs began to let him down. He had to keep an oxygen bottle in his house and he couldn't walk more than a few steps without gasping for air; it was heartbreaking to watch. I remember visiting him during his last year – he had just passed seventy – and he had obviously been reflecting on his life. I think I did alright, he said. I didn't have much of an education but I saw the world a bit and I became a Captain in the army. He looked around his little lounge, still arranged and ornamented just as Mum had left it, and went on. I know I didn't become a millionaire, but a man can only sit in one armchair, can't he?

The end came quickly, unexpectedly, and probably saved Dad from years of infirmity. One night he called Tony and said that he had a sharp pain in his stomach. It must have been bad, for him to do that. Tony arranged to get Dad straight into hospital in Taunton, rang around the family, and we congregated the next day at Dad's bedside. He had suffered a bleed in his duodenum, something that a surgeon could repair in a healthy man, but his lungs were too weak for anaesthesia. He's going to die, said the man in the white coat. That was that. The nurses would make Dad comfortable and, they told us, his kidneys would probably fail, leading him gently towards a coma.

When I had first arrived at the hospital Dad actually looked quite well, considering. He was flirting unashamedly with the young nurses, especially one who had caught his eye. The day went on - it was early August, hot and humid - and we three brothers chatted and came and went while Dad slipped away from us in small increments. He died in the early hours of the next morning, having been unconscious through most of the night.

Finding
contentment.

Wells, Somerset
in the late
seventies.

The love of
his life.

Mum, around
1980.

THIRTEEN

Some African cultures, I once read, don't lament the frailty of old age. They simply say that someone has seen too many summers. Dad saw seventy-one summers and I wish it had been more. He never met our daughter Ellie, born just three months after he died. He didn't live to see his great-grandchildren arrive and grow into their own lives.

He never got to use an iPad or a smartphone and I doubt that he ever heard of a man called Tony Blair. He never experienced the joy of the soap opera we call Brexit. He never saw men kissing men or women kissing women, nor the antics of the yellow-haired gentleman in the White House. He probably would have predicted the ascendant power of the Chinese. Well, he would say, there are so many of them aren't there? He might have struggled to imagine me, the baby, with white hair.

Beyond the circle of his family you could say that Dad's impact on the world was small. Like most of us, he simply witnessed events and got carried along by them. He hadn't started the war with Hitler but he was happy enough to do his bit. He didn't invent apartheid but he lived a part of his life within its rules. Other people, mostly anonymous, charted out the dismantling of British Africa while Dad made the best of it. He had no say in the matter when inflation gobbled up his savings.

That's not the whole picture, though. If you have seen Frank Capra's film It's a Wonderful Life you might think it is dated, sentimental tosh. It portrays a man, George Bailey, who contemplates suicide when he concludes that his life has been a failure. But when he is magically transported to visit an alternative world – a world where he had never been born - he learns to see how the lives of countless people would have been poorer without his small acts of courage and kindness and mercy.

Dad wasn't a perfect man but, like James Stewart's George, he touched a lot of lives. For Mum, often fragile and vulnerable, he was her foundation. He gave his sons equal portions of love. He, with Mum, opened his home to all and he rarely made enemies. He worked hard and set us an example to tell the truth and only take what we are due.

There would have been times, there are bound to be, when Dad didn't live up to these standards. Once or twice I saw him lose his temper, but it was rare. He would generally prefer a joke – however silly – to an argument.

And till the day he died, he consistently preferred Frank Sinatra to almost anyone. Especially Mick Jagger.

ACKNOWLEDGEMENTS

First, my thanks to my brother Stewart, my late brother Tony, and all the extended Bulls for providing those memories, pictures, anecdotes and explanations which helped me to piece together this brief account of Dad's life. Thanks also to Bill and Eileen Young, dear friends of my Mum and Dad during many years in Zambia.

For all things Royal Marines, thank you to Ken Guest. It was a privilege to meet you.

Through social media (thank you too, all you Facebook moderators) I was able to cast the net far beyond our immediate circle and connect with a range of people of many nationalities and races, each with their own African stories. I offer my thanks to those who took the time to speak to me, write to me or complete a questionnaire. As the book evolved it became apparent that very few of your individual stories would appear in print, but the opportunity to hear them developed my understanding of Dad's own experience and anchored the book in its historical context.

A number of you asked to remain anonymous but for the rest I have listed your names below, hoping that you might make your own connections and be inspired, perhaps, to put your stories on record. If I have missed anyone please accept my sincere apologies.

Finally, a huge thank you to Jude for putting up with the project, prodding my faltering memory and reading the drafts. I can't promise there won't be another one.

Claire Goodwin
Dawne Nissen
Edward Rybicki
Gary Clark
Gillian Simpson
Heather Sydenham
Hilary Broughton
Hillary Mulholland
Jacqueline Hayward
Jill Pearse
Jimmy Kotze
Jon Bourne
Josephine Wilson
Keith Hoets
Meena Ved

Michael Hart
Mike Bridgeford
Orla Jacobs
Peter Hall
Peter McLaren
Ray Still
Reginald Atkinson
Richard Stracey
Rory Whitaker
Rosemary Morgan
Sabrina Benanchietti
Sandra dos Santos
Sylvia Grove
Teresa van den Berg
Tim Stonehouse

READING

This book gave me an excuse to read. Many of the titles listed here are now out of print but can be obtained in original or e-book form without too much effort. I found AbeBooks particularly helpful www.abebooks.co.uk

David Kynaston – Austerity Britain 1945 - 51

Denys Blakeway - The Last Dance: 1936, The Year Our Lives Changed

Diana Polisensky – Whitewashed Jacarandas

Dominic Sandbrook - Never Had It So Good: A History of Britain from Suez to the Beatles

Dominic Sandbrook – State of Emergency: The Way We Were: Britain, 1970-1974

Dominic Sandbrook – Seasons in the Sun: The Battle for Britain, 1974-1979

Hardwicke Holderness – Lost Chance: Southern Rhodesia 1945 – 1958

Henry Kenney – Verwoerd

James D Ladd – By Sea, By Land: The Royal Marines 1919 - 1997

Judith Todd - Rhodesia

Kenneth Kaunda – Black Government?

Kenneth Kaunda – Zambia Shall Be Free

Michael and Maureen Harbott – Our Fine Romance

Mick Bond - From Northern Rhodesia to Zambia: Recollections of a DO/DC 1962-73

Pam Shurmer-Smith – Remnants of Empire

Richard Sampson – With Sword and Chain in Lusaka

Sir Roy Welensky – 4000 Days

William Tordoff (Editor) – Politics in Zambia.

THE WEB

As well as the inevitable Wikipedia there are many excellent online sites for research into the history, culture and politics of 20th century Central Africa. Here is a tiny sample:

The Northern Rhodesia Journal

http://www.spanglefish.com/northernrhodesiajournal/index.asp

Hansard records of UK parliamentary sittings

https://api.parliament.uk/historic-hansard/index.html

British Empire

https://www.britishempire.co.uk/article/fromnorthernrhodesiatozambia.htm

Colonial administration

http://www.spanglefish.com/gervasclay/

Zambia, memory and much more

https://remnantsofempire.com/

ABOUT THE AUTHOR

Timothy Bull spends much of his time working in aviation, which he does quite well, but prefers to play the ukulele, which he does quite badly.

His first novel The Visit is a transgalactic love story. It is available at the Amazon Kindle Store for half of the price of a cappuccino.